...es and miles,
...e groves...
...ivid gold of the orange,
...am with the exquisite
...ms the odor from which
...se to the very heavens.

ON JAMES
nia, 1910

Method of Fumigating Orange Orchard

way of Picking Oranges
Midwinter California

ange Groves and Snow Capped Mountains
from Smiley Heights, Redlands, Cal.

Xmas Greetings from California.
Instead of dodging snowballs
Which once I thought such fun
I'm sending you these oranges
Grown gold out here in the sun.

orange was a luxury
at the holiday season
but expensive exotic to
mas stockings
s and girls.

LYTHE
acific Business, 1937

I am Sending you a Box of Oranges from California

CALIFORNIA

Orange Blossoms.

...grant and fair, ...fume California's balmy air

...and Mountains.

I'll Eat Oranges for you if you'll throw Snowballs for me.

A Car Load of California Oranges.

Union Pacific 520

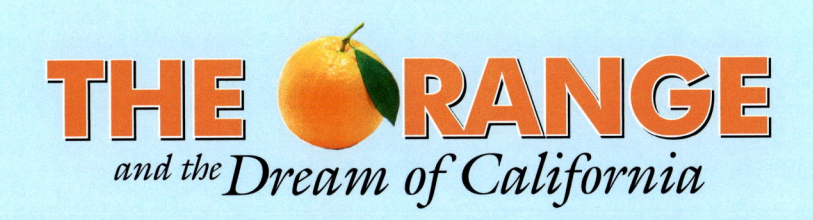

THE ORANGE
and the *Dream of California*

ACP
ANGEL CITY PRESS

THE ORANGE
and the *Dream of California*

David Boulé

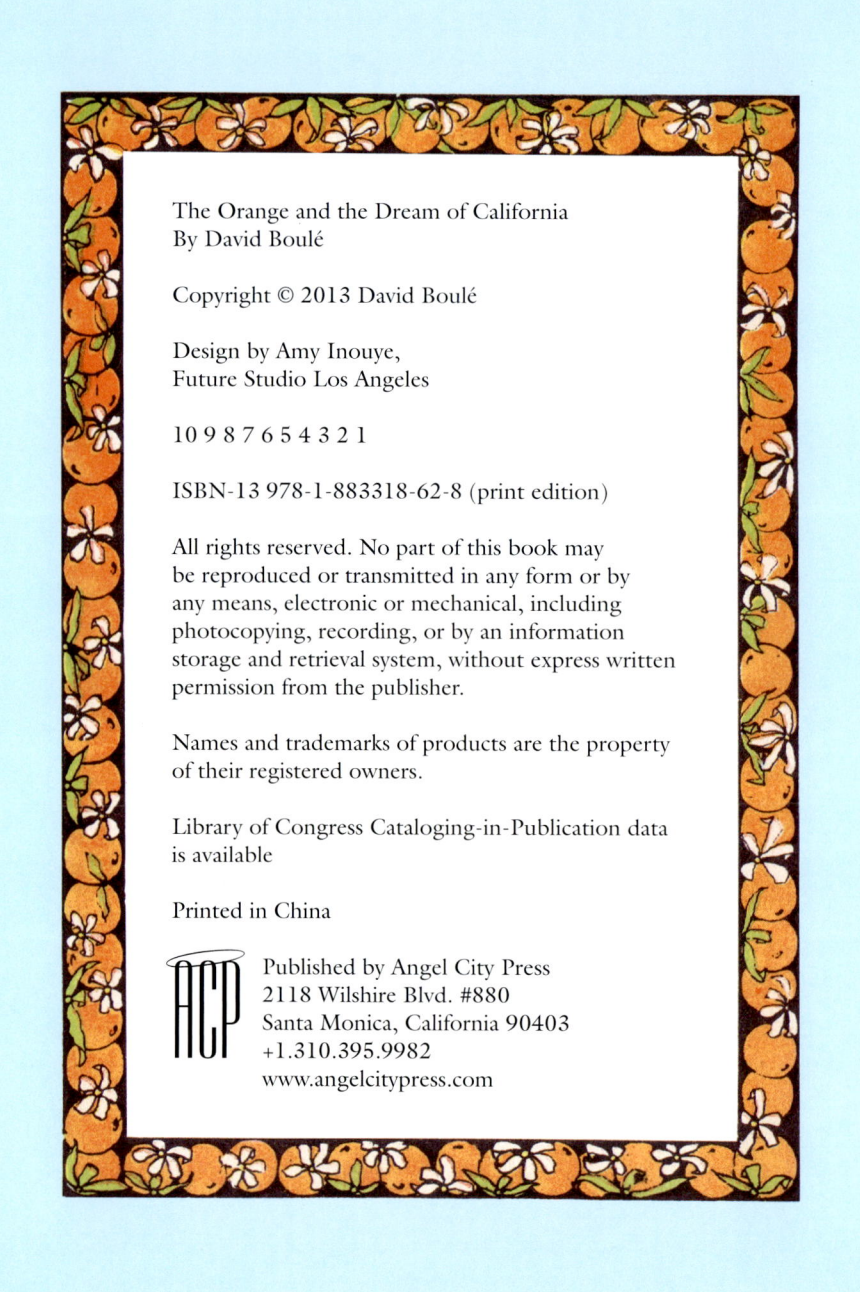

The Orange and the Dream of California
By David Boulé

Copyright © 2013 David Boulé

Design by Amy Inouye,
Future Studio Los Angeles

10 9 8 7 6 5 4 3 2 1

ISBN-13 978-1-883318-62-8 (print edition)

All rights reserved. No part of this book may be reproduced or transmitted in any form or by any means, electronic or mechanical, including photocopying, recording, or by an information storage and retrieval system, without express written permission from the publisher.

Names and trademarks of products are the property of their registered owners.

Library of Congress Cataloging-in-Publication data is available

Printed in China

Published by Angel City Press
2118 Wilshire Blvd. #880
Santa Monica, California 90403
+1.310.395.9982
www.angelcitypress.com

To my wife Marcia, for her boundless love and encouragement and to our son Henry, who showed me the way to scholarship.

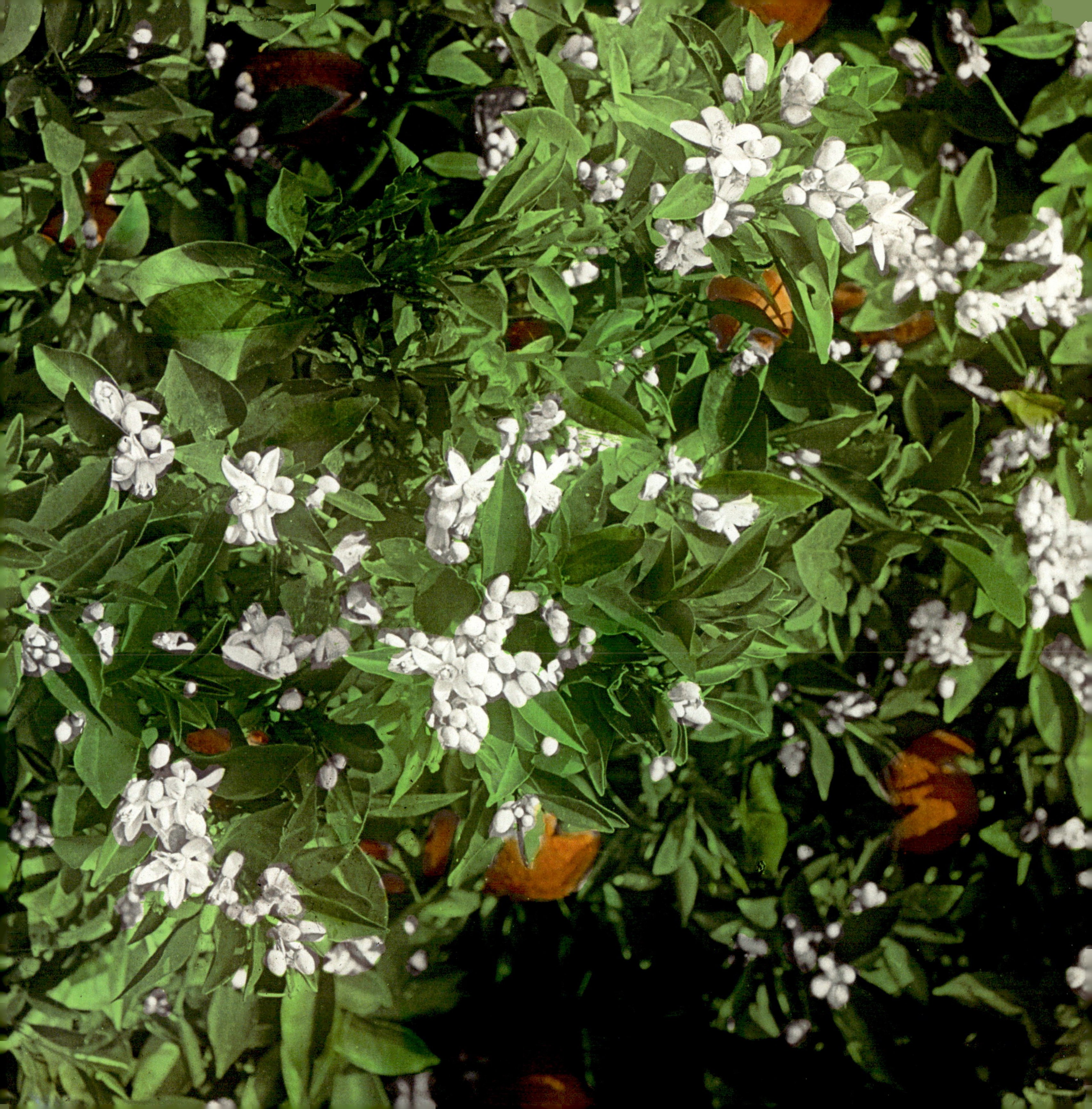

*In the full of spring on the banks of a river—
Two big gardens planted with thousands of orange trees.
Their thick leaves are putting the clouds to shame.*
Du Fu
poet, eighth century

*Know ye that on the right hand of the Indies there is an island called California,
very close to the Terrestrial Paradise.*
Garci Rodríguez del Montalvo
author, *The Exploits of Esplandián,* sixteenth century

California is a fine place to live, if you happen to be an orange.
Fred Allen
radio personality, twentieth century

Contents

Introduction 11

1 The Romance of the Orange 13

2 The Dream of California 21

3 Destiny—The Orange in California 31

4 California's Real Gold Rush—
   The Sunkist Story 49

5 Fantasyland—
   Expositions and Orange Shows 75

6 Love's Labour's Lost—
   The People, Skills, Machines and Hard Work
   Needed to Bring Paradise to the Table 87

7 Picture Perfect—
   Orange Crate Labels 117

8 *Ready for its Close-up—*
The Orange in Hollywood **127**

9 *Words and Music—*
Poems and Songs for California's Orange **133**

10 *Every Picture Tells a Story—*
Snapshots of the Dream **141**

11 *Tourists, Trolleys, and Trains* **147**

12 *A Little Bit of Paradise for the Folks Back Home—*
California Orange Souvenirs **157**

13 *Paradise Lost—*
From Land of Enchantment to Suburban Plenty **165**

NOTES **169**
BIBLIOGRAPHY **170**
IMAGE CREDITS **174**
ACKNOWLEDGMENTS **175**

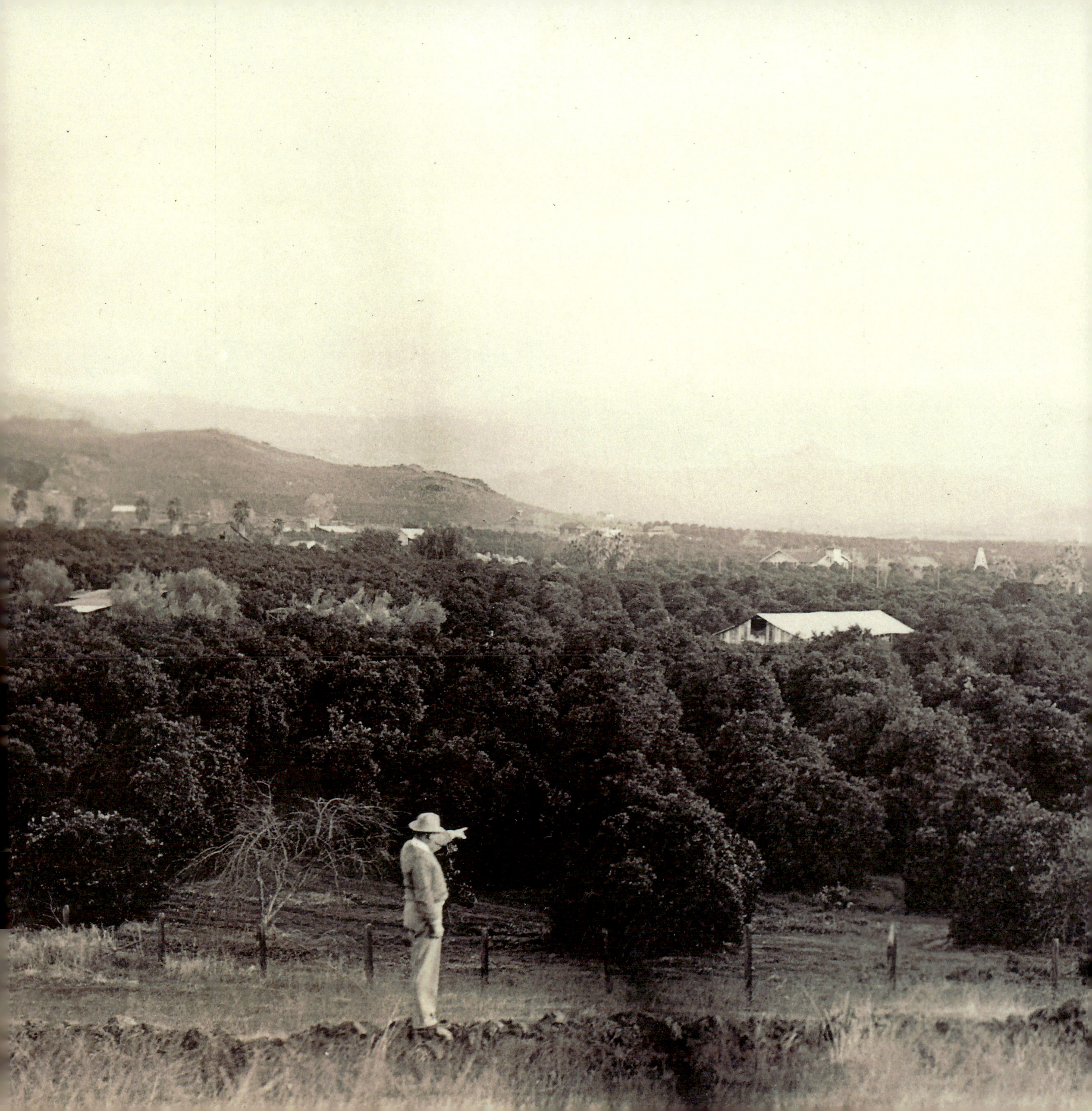

Introduction

This book is about romance and dreams, the romance and dreams surrounding the orange and California, and how these two have swirled together for hundreds of years. The image of California as paradise and the orange as unique among all fruit endures because, partially, these things are true. Recognized by chroniclers, journalists, scientists, growers, and other objective observers, these traits have then been magnified by poets and boosters, artists and hucksters, songwriters and bureaucrats—with both artistic and commercial motivation—to appeal to people's continuing desire to believe that such exceptional perfection can really exist.

This is not a comprehensive history of the orange industry in California—that subject has been covered in many excellent books. California is not Eden, the orange is not a miracle, and the orange industry has faced challenges and controversy. This book does not seek to fully explore, deny, or gloss over any of this. Its focus, instead, is on how these two evocative entities and symbols—the orange and California—have built on one another for centuries to feed the imagination and conjure a compelling fantasy, like Brigadoon, that nurtures our universal desire for beauty, health, enchantment, reinvention, and peace.

Sandro Botticelli was commissioned to paint Primavera, or Allegory of Spring, *for the marriage of a Medici. A work abundant with symbolism, Botticelli used orange blossoms to represent chastity and oranges fertility. Similar imagery continued into the Victorian age.*

1

The Romance of the Orange

*He hangs in shades the orange bright,
Like golden lamps in a green night*

Bermudas
Andrew Marvell, 1621-1678
English poet

The apricot is wonderful, but doesn't conjure fantasy or call to the gods. The cherry is exquisite, but has no mystery. The apple is, well, just the thing we eat one of every day. But the orange, it has it all—flamboyant color, exuberant taste, intoxicating flowers, provocative reproduction, endless variety, a global story and the sweep of history. The orange is the stuff of legends.

The ancients believed in The Garden of Hesperides, a grove of immortality-granting "golden apples," located somewhere in the far western corner of the world (California, perhaps?). After completing his first ten labors, Hercules was given two more, one of which was to steal fruit from this garden of bliss tended by nymphs. The golden apples of Hesperides are often portrayed in art as oranges and, in fact, botanists classify all citrus as "hesperidia."

In the 1482 painting *Primavera*, Sandro Botticelli depicts a group of mythological figures, including Venus and a *putto*, emerging from an orange grove. The orange trees form an arc over Venus's head, suggesting that she's emerging from a temple, while The Three Graces dance and Mercury protects them all. Cool.

Cloaked in mystery, available only to the elite until modern times, the orange has been known as the fruit of gods, the food of emperors, a token of gratitude, and a symbol of health, wealth, and love. It's quite a story.

"The history of the spread of citrus reads like a

romance," says the otherwise staid and academic standard reference work on the botany and culture of citrus.[1] The first recorded mention of any type of citrus fruit dates back more than four thousand years, and there have been many scholarly investigations into its origin and migration over the centuries. This has involved real sleuthing, keen imagination, and some controversy. From deciphering archaic poems, literature, and descriptions to discern what's really being talked about—is the reference to a citron, an orange, a lemon, something else?—to analyzing ancient art in the attempt to confirm where and when the many types of citrus were grown as they moved around the world, researchers still work to create a definitive map of the migration of citrus across time and continents.

A Roman mosaic in Valencia, Spain, illustrating the Twelve Labors portrays Hercules stealing the golden apples from the Garden of the Hesperides.

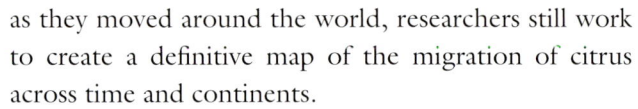

Here's what we know. The ancestors of all the citrus we love today originated in "southeastern Asia, the East Indian Archipelago, New Guinea, Melanesia, New Caledonia, and Australia."[2] Precisely when and what the first types were like is murky, but only moderate changes were required to create our contemporary varieties. Less than a handful of prototype species may account for the thousands of cultivated varieties known today. This is because citrus mutates readily—sometimes several varieties can exist on a single tree—and hybridizes easily. The superb essayist John McPhee relates in his 1966 book *Oranges* this incredible experiment:

Researchers Philip C. Reece and J.F.L. Childs cut up eighteen hundred and eighty-five Persian limes and found no seeds at all. So they went to a concentrate plant and filled two dump trucks with pulp from tens of thousands of Persian limes, which had just been turned into limeade. Picking through it all by hand, they found two hundred and fifty seeds, and planted them. Up from those lime seeds came sweet oranges, bitter orange trees, grapefruit trees, lemon trees, tangerines, limequats, citrons—and two seedlings that proved to be Persian limes . . . . A citrus seed will tend to sprout a high proportion of . . . nucellar seedlings, which are asexually produced and always

14 The Orange and the Dream of California

In Lord Frederic Leighton's The Garden of the Hesperides, *Greek mythology melds with the Old Testament's Eden; goddesses wait to tempt while a single serpent lingers.*

Technically classified as a hesperidia, *a kind of berry, the orange belongs to the genus* Citrus, *the family* Rutaceae. *The orange today is the most commonly grown tree fruit in the world.* Citrus Aurantium, *pictured above, is known as the Seville orange, the sour or bitter orange. Sour oranges were the first to find their way out of Asia and into the Middle East and Europe.*

have the exact characteristics of the plant from which the seed came. The seeds of the Persian limes, however, sent up a high proportion of zygotic seedlings . . . that arise from a fertilized egg cell. If zygotic seedlings come from parents that are true species, the seedlings will always . . . resemble one or the other parent, or both. If zygotic seedlings come from parents that are hybrids, they can resemble almost any kind of citrus ever known.

Crazy-quilt botany is just a tiny part of how and why citrus has journeyed around the world and been so coveted wherever it has gone.

Each of the major varieties—the citron, lemon, sour orange, and sweet orange—migrated individually and on their own timetable. The citron was first. Its value as a perfume and food flavoring, and the newly developing commerce between far-flung civilizations, encouraged its westward travel. Excavations have uncovered four-thousand-year-old citron seeds in Mesopotamia. That's where, in 334 BC, the botanical experts traveling with Alexander the Great found the "Persian Apple" and brought it back to the Mediterranean. Soon cultivated by Greek and Jewish settlers around the eastern

The Romance of the Orange

15

Mediterranean, the citron was, in time, incorporated into the Jewish Feast of Tabernacles, and was even featured on a Jewish coin from the first century AD.

Ah, but we are here to talk about the orange. John McPhee has suggested that the migration of the orange "closely and sometimes exactly kept pace with the major journeys of civilization." Pierre Laszlo, in *Citrus: A History*, goes further:

> Let me throw in a strange idea, both irrational and improvable. The proposition is that nature carries culture with it. The seeds of a plant somehow ferry, in their genes, as it were, aspects of a civilization that deemed that particular plant important. I shall assert more specifically—although I won't prove it, since such a proposition is devoid of any factual support—that orange trees connect the French Sun King, Louis XIV, to the emperor of China across the centuries.[3]

China mastered the cultivation of the sweet orange centuries before it reached Europe, as far back as 2500 B.C. Oranges are specifically mentioned in the *Five Classics*, a compendium of Confucian thought from about 500 BC.

As ancient empires rose and fell, civilizations collided, merged, and evolved. By the first century AD, the wealthy citizens in Rome were willing to spend extravagantly for exotic delicacies from faraway regions, foods almost beyond their imaginations. Imported oranges from the east were probably among these delicacies. Some historians recognize orange trees in mosaics from Pompeii and other early cities in Italy, indicating that perhaps trees, and not just fruit, had made the westward journey by that time, too. Most scholars agree, however, that regardless of the precise timetable, the sour orange traveled first, and the sweet orange followed a few centuries later. Some also suggest that early transplanted trees were grown, but were unable to produce fruit.

Within a relatively short period of time, historically speaking, of course, orchards of oranges and lemons were being grown in the near east and southern Europe. While the Bible makes no specific mention of any citrus fruit, proof of the orange's advance and cultivation is in a fourth-century mausoleum built by Constantine; an early Christian mosaic shows oranges, along with other citrus, on branches surrounded by leaves.

Citrus was thriving and important in the Middle East by the first century AD, as indicated by its prominent depiction on the currency of that period. This bronze coin from the Jewish war against Rome features the image of an Etrog, a type of citron.

The oranges of the island are like blazing fire
Amongst the emerald boughs
ABDUR-RAHMAN IBN MUHAMMED IBN OMAR
Fourteenth century

With the fall of Rome, the emerging Muslim empire reached further into South Asia, Asia, and Africa than had its predecessor, expanding trade and bringing, among many other items, additional types of citrus cultivation to the Near East, the Mediterranean rim, and even the southern part of the Iberian Peninsula. Arabic literature contains frequent mentions of the orange and other citrus fruits, and this is where the word "orange" emerges. In Sanskrit, the fruit was called *naranga*. This evolved in Persian to *naranj*, becoming *naranja* in Spanish and eventually *orange* in French. Over time, these gave the orange its own name, replacing centuries of referring to the fruit as a "Chinese apple."

In the eleventh century, the Crusades extended the desire for the orange further into Europe. With the Renaissance and the Age of Discovery, traders from Genoa, Portugal, and Spain reached India and Asia by sea and brought back ever-newer varieties of oranges. Sailors planted oranges and other citrus trees along trade routes to ward off scurvy. The demand for the sour orange quickly faded with the appearance of superior varieties of the sweet orange.

Folio from Aja'ib al-makhluqat (Wonders of Creation) by Muhammad al-Qazvini, ca. 1203-1283.

In the early sixteenth century, the Dominican historian Leandro Alberti described in *Descrizione di tutta Italia* "immense plantations of orange, lemon, and citron"[4] trees throughout Italy. Michel de Nostradamus, the healer and French apothecary best known today as a doomsday seer, published in 1552 *Traité des fardemens*, which offered recipes for making cosmetics, candy, and potions from oranges and orange blossoms. The orange was fast garnering a reputation as special, valuable, and desirable—not just as a food, but as a symbol.

French kings visiting Italy coveted the cache of citrus and returned determined to grow it as an emblem of power. The French climate was not-at-all suited to orange cultivation, so by the fourteenth century nobility had developed glass-walled, heated buildings, called *les orangeries* just for growing citrus. Louis XIV had the best, of course, at Versailles. He wasn't called the Sun King for nothing. For the next two hundred years, oranges would be the exclusive property of the aristocracy and the wealthy.

There is no citrus species indigenous to the New World. When the Turkish Empire

The Romance of the Orange

*Just recently there has been sent to Rome . . .
from Lisbon a beautiful tree with golden fruit.
Some say the tree has come originally from China . . . .
It surpasses others [in] that a crushed leaf smells more alluring . . .
The fruit is round in shape with a skin . . .
most glowingly and delightfully yellow . . .
The pulp and juice are so golden in color one would think
gold had been melted away into its juice.*[5]

GIOVANNI BATTISTA FERRARI, 1646

sealed off land routes to India, Columbus's plan to reach there by sailing west towards the orange sun—head west to go to the east?—was just one of the theories to find new routes being investigated by major European trading nations and city-states. On his second voyage, Columbus commanded seventeen ships and brought with him everything needed to establish permanent settlements, including seeds for oranges, lemons, and citrons.

Soon, all Spanish sailors sailing west were required to carry one hundred citrus seeds with them, and it wasn't long before oranges and other citrus were growing wild throughout the Caribbean and the coast of South America.

The orange had come to the Americas.

The aristocrat of fruit. Planted in massive containers, the orange trees at Versailles were rolled out into the sun during summer months and then back into a glass-fronted, opulent orangerie during the inhospitable winter to be protected and pampered, the perfect symbol of power and prestige. This depiction was painted in 1794 by Jean-Baptiste Hilaire.

The Orange and the Dream of California

The Magical Marvelous Orange Tree

Jean Eugène Robert-Houdin was a clockmaker, inventor, illusionist, and magician, born in 1805 in Blois, France, the son of a master watchmaker. His interest in art, magic, performing, and mechanics led him to revolutionize the way magic was presented; he wore formal clothes, he arranged his performances so one trick led to an even bigger surprise, and he helped establish the practice of performing in theaters. American magician Ehrich Weiss changed his name to Harry Houdini, and adopted the stage name Houdini after reading Robert-Houdin's autobiography.

One of Robert-Houdin's most famous tricks involved an automaton and was called *The Marvelous Orange Tree*. An egg, a lemon, and an orange were positioned on stage. Robert-Houdin would ask a woman in the audience for a handkerchief, which he would make disappear; along with the egg, lemon, and orange. All that was left was a fine powder, which he put into a vial, mixed with alcohol, and set on fire.

An assistant then rolled a small, barren orange tree into view. Robert-Houdin would place the flame under the tree, causing orange blossoms to appear. With a wave of his wand, the blossoms became oranges. To prove the fruit was real, he picked the oranges one-by-one and tossed them to the audience. When only one orange was left on the tree, Robert-Houdin waved his wand again, causing the last orange, a mechanical one, to split into quarters, and two motorized butterflies to emerge from behind the tree. The butterflies dipped into the open orange and pulled up the spectator's handkerchief!

The Marvelous Orange Tree still exists. Refurbished by the celebrated builder of equipment for magicians, John Gaughan, it was demonstrated on British magician Paul Daniels' television show. The *Orange Tree* illusion was featured in Steven Millhauser's short story "Eisenheim The Illusionist," which became the basis for the 2006 film *The Illusionist*.

The Romance of the Orange

"The early history of California . . . reads like a fairy tale,"
states a 1922 history tome San Bernardino and Riverside Counties: With Selected Biography of Actors and Witnesses.
This map was produced by Dutch cartographer Johannes Vingboons in about 1650.

The Dream of California

California...
promises to become to the United States what Greece was to ancient Europe.
Harry Ellington Brook
The Land of Sunshine: Southern California—
An authentic description of its natural features, resources and prospects. 1893

When Carey McWilliams wrote in his 1949 book *California: The Great Exception* that there was something about California that has always "incited hyperbole," he was referring to five hundred years of "tricks, deceptions, and wondrous visions" going back to a time before a single European had set foot here. In the late fifteenth century, Garci Rodríguez del Montalvo wrote *Las Sergas de Esplandian* (*The Exploits of Esplandian*). His hero visits an island named for Queen Calafia, an imposing and beautiful Amazon. Historian Kevin Starr beautifully captured this collision of fantasy and history when he said, "California entered history as a myth." The mythmaking has continued at high volume ever since.

A land fictionalized as overflowing with gold and pearls and striking women was enough to motivate Hernando Cortés and other early Spanish explorers to look in earnest for this extraordinary place. No one knows which adventurer first coined the word "California," but it is certain that the assumptions that the place was an island and within easy sailing distance of Asia delayed recognition of California's true value. Looking for what wasn't here blinded them to what was.

Even the trees and plants did not belong here.
They came, like the people, from far places, some familiar, some exotic,
all wanderers of one sort or another seeking peace or fortune
or the last frontier, or a thousand dreams of escape.[6]

FRANK FENTON
A Place in the Sun, 1942

FACT, FICTION; OPPORTUNITY, OPPORTUNISM

When Franciscan missionaries arrived in Alta California in 1769 and built the now-fabled chain of missions, they laid the foundation for the next key component of California's image. The Spanish missions, built to colonize and secure Spain's claim to the area and constructed primarily with forced labor, worked in conjunction with the area's natural beauty to give a uniquely California look to the ancient concept of Arcadia. When Mexico won its independence from Spain in 1821, the new government ordered all Spanish-born residents to leave—including most of the missionaries. The native-born *Californios* assumed control, modeling themselves after the landed gentry of Spain, living cloistered, easygoing, privileged lives growing wheat and raising cattle—growing oranges for commerce was several decades away—on baronial-sized ranchos, each consisting of hundreds of square miles. But this storied era of Zorro and the Cisco Kid lasted less than twenty-five years.

The United States declared war on Mexico on May 13, 1846 and, just four years later, California became the thirty-first state in the Union. The rancho period was dismissed and forgotten by the energetic Yankees who flooded in and saw the soil and sun, the water and wide-open space, the ports and mountain passes, and shouted "Eureka," this is it!

The mission and rancho periods added an architectural sense of place and an easily romanticized and picturesque lifestyle to

The Orange and the Dream of California

> *It is a land of solid realities and glittering frauds...*
> *When you stay long enough to see them and find out that the country*
> *is not to blame for your overwrought imagination, the unwise enthusiasm*
> *of friends or the deliberate lies of others, you will begin to like it.*
>
> THEODORE S. VAN DYKE
> *Southern California,* 1886

the area's already-established reputation for a temperate climate and natural abundance. And they eventually provided a convenient "pre-history" onto which others would project their own values and meanings, casting "a spell of enchantment—a daydream of California" that influenced how California projected itself, giving "the state some of its most salient myths."[7]

Fed by a flood of books, magazine pieces, art, photographs, and motion pictures, California's past and promise—real and imagined—became a subject of fascination for Americans in the frozen and rapidly industrializing East. While *Ramona* (1884) was the first novel and, far and away, the most influential, the exploration and reinterpretation of California's past began a decade earlier. New York journalist Charles Nordoff established California as a tourist destination when his *California for Health, Wealth and Residence* was published in 1871. Nordhoff's work was underwritten by the railroads, using it to encourage travel, and his book played a significant role in starting California's first housing boom.. Elizabeth Hughes added to California's growing reputation as a place of reinvention and enchantment with *The California of the Padres; or Footprints of Ancient Communism*. She dedicated the book to "all those whose interest in the present of our noble State, and hopes for its rapidly unfolding future, lead them to look back at its singular and remarkable past." She added, "Nature has prepared the place for a laboratory of new ideas, and a new social order."[8]

Themes of abundance, health, civility, culture,

This image was used on a 1920s postcard promoting the sale of industrial citrus oils. Even when selling commercial products, the myth of an idealized, exotic, peacefully agrarian California was utilized. The original of this painting hangs in the executive offices of Sunkist.

The Dream of California

A Road by Any Other Name

The original artery connecting the missions was a simple dirt trail, but in keeping with the larger-than-life California way, it was named *El Camino Real*, "The Royal Road." Even today it is often referred to as the King's Highway. There *was* something beautiful and special about "El Camino Real." In an era when signage was nonexistent, the padres scattered mustard seed along both sides to differentiate the mission road from others. Not quite the yellow bricks of Oz, but the brilliant, waving, golden flowers of the mustard must have added a welcoming and atmospheric character to the path as it wove its way over California's coastal hills and past native oaks.

"America's most beautiful 400 miles" states this 1935 souvenir map of El Camino Real, *the road connecting the California missions.*

climate, contentment, and a vigorous-but-easy-going kind of work ethic permeate books like *Life in California Before the Conquest* (1846), *Three Years in California* (1850), *Southern California: Its Valleys, Hills, Streams; Its Animals, Birds, and Fishes; Its Gardens, Farms and Climate* (1886) and *Adobe Days* (1925).

The orange, of course, was often a key subject or character in many of these works, and was equally glorified. In 1885, William Andrew Spalding wrote *The Orange, Its Culture in California*. "Orange culture must continue as it has begun, an industry suited to the most intelligent and refined people . . . . As it requires both skill and industry, it gives healthful occupation to the mind as well as the body."[9] Byron Martin Lelong added his *A Treatise on Citrus Culture in California* in 1888. Summing-up such sentiment was Edward James Wickson in *California Garden-flowers* (1915), who wrote, "California stands clear in the eyes of the world as the point most desirable to attain . . . the fullest joys of living."[10]

As Kevin Starr noted, "Lest such evocations be dismissed as mere ballyhoo, it must be said that in the thirty years that followed these predictions, much of what was envisioned came true. Rarely, if ever . . . has such beauty and civility, such luxuriance and orderly repose been achieved on an American landscape as that brought about by citrus on the landscape of Southern California."

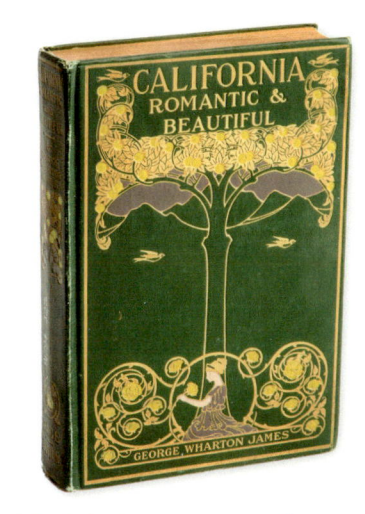

With a sheltering orange tree on its cover, this 1914 California travel guide included all the California tropes: idealized Native Americans, romanticizing of the Spanish and Mexican periods, exultation of the natural environment, and health faddism.

Motion pictures, a medium built on melodrama, fantasy, and idealized images, discovered California and its storytelling potential early and began adding to its fairytale image. Mary Pickford starred in D.W. Griffth's California-themed *The Thread of Destiny* in 1910. *In Old California*, *The Way of the World*, and *Over Silent Paths* soon followed, all set in the era of the missions or ranchos. *Ramona* alone was filmed five times, in 1910 with Mary Pickford, 1928 with Delores del Rio, 1936 starring Loretta Young, in 1959 with Raquel Tejada (soon to be Raquel Welch), and then again in 1969 with Anne Archer. And although their scripts were set in the film noir world of the 1930s and '40s, even writers as hardboiled as Raymond Chandler and James M. Cain were sucker-punched by California's charms, waxing poetic about the California climate, plenty, and possibilities.

Five centuries of such storytelling had a cumulative effect largely because, other than that bit about Amazons, there is *some* truth or historical underpinning to all of California's myths and exaggerated charms. And often, it's been substantial. Take California's reputation as a place of plenty. In the sixteenth and seventeenth centuries, nearly one-third of *all* Native Americans in

. . . not even the drenched darkness could hide the flawless lines of the orange trees.
RAYMOND CHANDLER
The Big Sleep, 1939

The Dream of California

*With this peaceable life, possibly in part as a result of it,
there has grown up in the people an intense love of their land . . . .
Further out (houses) become villas,
set down in the midst of plantations of orange and lemon . . .
which have a mysterious and attractive quality.
They are our dreamed-of orange groves.*
"Southern California—III," *Harper's* magazine, December, 1882

We had met with settlements of pretty Spanish names, with old missions, with Mexican leather breeches and jingling spurs, with vineyards, and raisin-making, and occasional orange and palm trees . . . . The country is older, the Spanish names more musical; the orange and lemon are not grown . . . for ornament simply, but as a principal crop. The climate is of a genial mildness which draws hither the greater number of all those who seek California for health.
"Paradise"—by C.S. Reinhart and C.A. Vanderhoof,
Harper's *magazine, December, 1882*

the United States lived in California. With abundant food, they developed communal societies and had little need to war with their neighbors. Mild weather meant shelter was easy. With sufficient food and shelter, there was leisure. "The rhythms of daily life, the pageant of nature . . . fixed for them a place in the world"[11] very much like that envisioned by the Greeks in their distant, mythic realm of Arcadia—a land like California, isolated from the rest of world, its citizens in harmony with an unspoiled nature . . . and happy.

In the late nineteenth century, as cities choked with people and factories, and new mass media brought information and quackery to its masses, the climate and promise of California lured thousands to the state, all desperate for better health. Carey McWilliams wrote: "To appreciate the enthusiasm of the early tourists for the climate of Southern California, it should be recalled that, in the 'sixties, 'seventies, and 'eighties, there was more incipient and chronic invalidism in America than one can possibly imagine today . . . Reading lush accounts of the climate of Southern California, these ailing Middle Westerners set forth in droves for the promised land."

Fantasists, adventurers, proselytizers, those looking to better the world, those looking to better

The Orange and the Dream of California

Pulp Fiction—
Ramona: How One Book Built the Dream

One book changed California forever. The most significant literary contributor to the creation of an idealized, early California history was the first one written: the 1884 novel *Ramona*.

Helen Hunt Jackson, a native of Massachusetts and a life-long friend of Emily Dickinson, was a prolific, crusading author who, several years earlier, had written *A Century of Dishonor*, which detailed abuses against Native Americans by the federal government. After several vacation visits to California, she became smitten with the collapsing walls, empty bell towers, and abandoned gardens of the missions and began work on a novel she hoped would, like *Uncle Tom's Cabin*, "set forth some Indian experiences in a way to move people's hearts."[12]

The book changed California, but not in the ways she intended.

An earnest attempt to highlight the mistreatment of the area's Native Americans, the book became a phenomenal bestseller with its sentimental, melodramatic story that transformed the region's Indians into pre-Raphaelite creations and recast the *Californios* as Euro-style aristocrats. The book was released just as railroads were promoting California as a winter vacation destination for Midwesterners and those in the East.

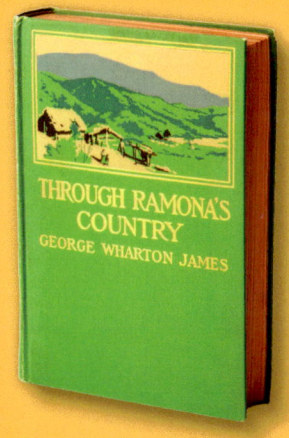

Somewhat like Charles Fletcher Lummis, George Wharton James was a journalist and author who focused on the American southwest and California. One of his most popular books was the travel guide Through Ramona's Country, *published in 1909. While he acknowledges in the introduction that* Ramona *is "fiction," he insists that the book ". . . is more true than fact(s)."*

An entire industry developed overnight to package "Ramona's land," with tours to the "real" locations in the novel. Plays and pageants and numerous books—both novels and travel guides—helped jumpstart the first of California's real estate booms.

This rediscovered California "history" was unrecognizable from what had actually occured. *Ramona* recast every aspect of early California, fabricating new, romantic forgeries. And while *Ramona* was embraced, real Native Americans continued to be marginalized and kept from participating in the state's growing economy.

Ramona's influence continues; the book has been the source for five motion pictures and has never been out of print.

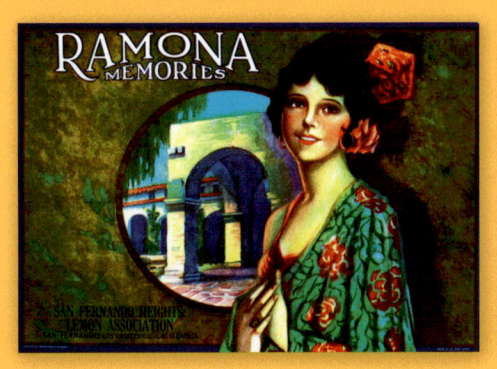

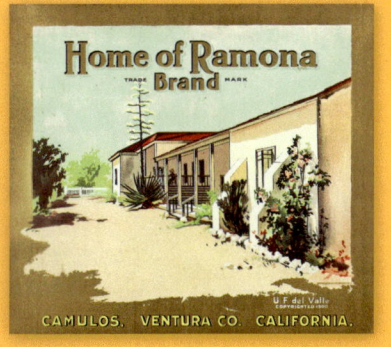

The Dream of California

27

> *I met a Californian who would*
> *Talk California—a state so blessed,*
> *He said, in climate none had ever died there*
> *A natural death*
>
> ROBERT FROST

themselves, first-rate artists and first-rate hucksters, the Gold Rush, the transcontinental railroad, boom-and-bust real estate, a growing population, and a changing world—they all came together in California. Carey McWilliams summarized this boiling brew when he said "there is a golden haze over the land—the dust of gold is in the air."[13] Many others have elaborated on this description of the Golden State, adding the golden nugget, the golden poppy, the Golden Gate, the black gold of oil, golden sunshine and golden dreams. And the golden orange was poised to be the symbol of it all.

Charles Chester Pierce opened a photo studio in Los Angeles about 1900 and worked for three decades assembling images—taken by others and himself—of California. The breadth of subjects covered, along with the artistic and often-romanticized techniques used, made his collection popular with researchers and boosters alike. This 1895 image, with oranges glowing in the trees, is titled "Alessandro Waiting for Ramona."

The Orange and the Dream of California

Of all the trees that man has corseted to uniform "symmetry" and fattened for his use, none other is more beautiful and no more grateful (than the orange).
CHARLES FLETCHER LUMMIS
Out West, 1903

California's Colorful Champion

Beginning in the 1880s, popular media was filled with idealizations and exclamations about California, its romantic past and its promising future. The words of praise were accompanied by lovely, evocative paintings, drawings, and photographs. *Land of Sunshine,* renamed *Out West* in 1901, was one of these media boosters. The magazine was edited for more than a decade by Charles Fletcher Lummis. Lummis dropped out of Harvard in his senior year, taking a newspaper job in Cincinnati. When offered a job as the first City Editor of the *Los Angeles Times,* he chose to walk two thousand miles to his new employment. Later, after moving to New Mexico and working as a freelance writer, he was shot but not killed by an assassin hired by local corrupt officials. Married twice and divorced by both wives for his infidelities, Lummis was a poet, author, librarian, adventurer, and Indian-rights advocate. He also established the Southwest Indian Museum and was a leader in the movement to restore California's missions. Lummis is perhaps the best known—but just one—of the many ambitious nonconformists whose passionate interests and outsized personalities shaped California's image.

The Dream of California

With its view from Mt. Rubidoux onto the abundant orchards of Riverside, this image was captured by Howard Clinton Tibbitts who worked as a photographer for the Southern Pacific Railroad for forty years, beginning in 1892. His photographs were used to promote travel to California, and often appeared in the railroad's Sunset *magazine.*

Destiny—
The Orange in California

That the culture of the citrus family of fruits is destined to become one of the leading industries of the great State of California is no longer disputed by the intelligent, reflective, progressive mind.

THOMAS A. GAREY
Orange Culture in California, 1882

FROM SMALL THINGS, BIG THINGS ONE DAY COME— THE ORANGE ARRIVES IN CALIFORNIA

The eventual California citrus cornucopia filled slowly. There were no oranges in California before Franciscan padres planted seeds they brought with them in 1769, when they established Mission San Diego de Acala, the first of the chain. But it was years before the first homegrown California orange was actually picked and eaten, since an orange tree can take up to a decade to produce fruit when grown from seed.

Mission San Gabriel Arcángel, the fourth in the chain that would eventually number twenty-one, holds the honor of having the first sizable grove of California oranges, undoubtedly grown from the seeds of those first trees planted in San Diego. In the 1880s, journalists who interviewed elderly Franciscan fathers established that the San Gabriel grove was most likely planted about 1804. The orchard was modest in size, but the seeds from its trees were the source for much of early California's subsequent success. The last of those first California orange trees died in the early-twentieth century. They'd lived more than one hundred years.

When you come to a place that not only thinks it has a destiny, but knows it has a destiny, you cannot but be arrested . . . In short, it is going to be a paradise on earth.
                          James M. Cain
                     "Paradise" *The American Mercury*, 1933

Orchards outside mission compounds weren't established until after secularization. In 1834, a Frenchman, Jean Louis Vignes, bought thirty-five sweet orange trees from Mission San Gabriel and moved them several miles west to his property on the outskirts of El Pueblo de Nuestra Señora la Reina de los Ángeles, a dusty, drowsy village of low-lying buildings and a few hundred people. This was the second California orange orchard. But with a small, disbursed population and a culture disinclined toward commerce, the orange remained uncommon and unconsidered. When John C. Fremont swept into California in 1846, during the tumultuous period when the United States was wrestling California from Mexico, he observed that "little remains of the orchards that were kept in high cultivation at the Missions."[14]

As has happened so often in California's history and the development of its bounty, it took a transplant to see the real promise of the orange in California. William Wolfskill's family had been Daniel Boone's neighbors in Kentucky. As a young man, Wolfskill left home to find his fortune and become a fur trapper. Landing in California in 1831—traveling from New Mexico and helping establish what would later become known as the Old Spanish Trail—he became a naturalized Mexican citizen, bought land, and married. Securing sweet

"This piece of wood is genuine California redwood" reads the back of this 1941 postcard. From home of the tallest trees in the world to the place best known for the mythical, magical orange, California was promoted as growing the biggest and best.

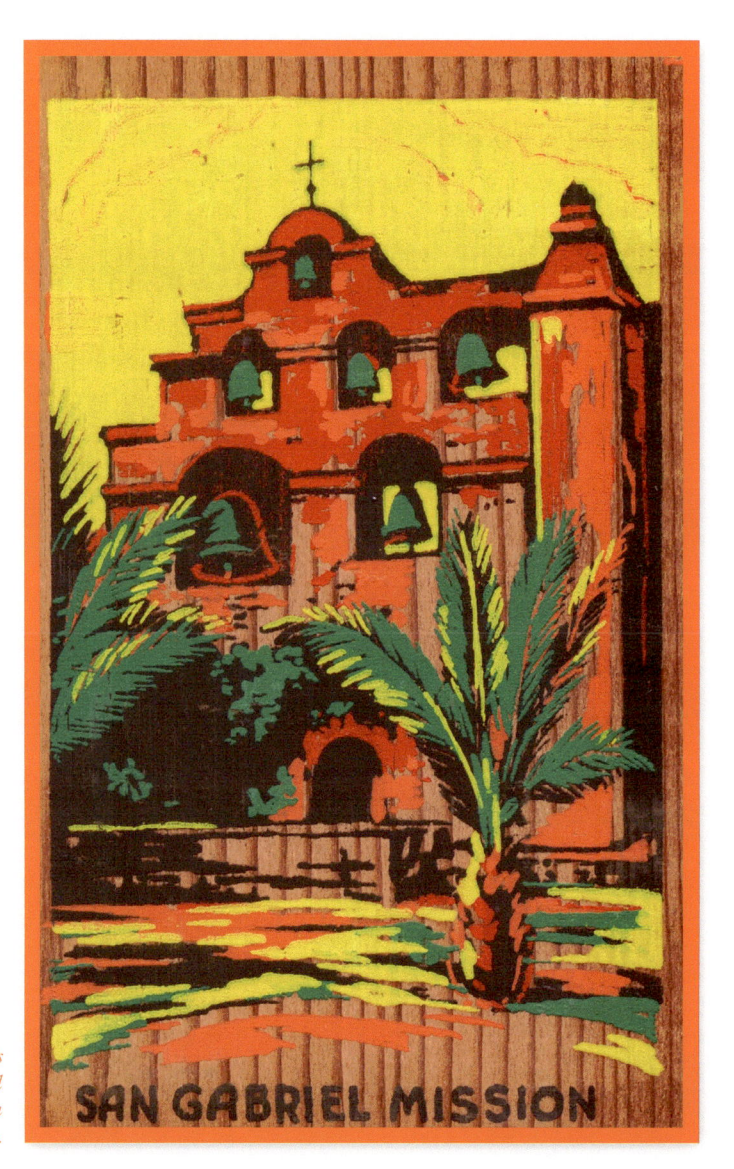

32

The Orange and the Dream of California

> **To own an orange grove in Southern California
> is to live on the real gold coast of American agriculture.**
> CAREY MCWILLIAMS
> *Southern California: An Island on the Land,* 1946

A committee of the California State Agricultural Society toured Southern California in 1858 and found only seven citrus orchards. As late as 1870 there were only 8,000 orange trees in Los Angeles County and fewer than 35,000 statewide. This image is from William Makepeace Thayer's Marvels of the New West: A Vivid Portrayal of the Stupendous Marvels in the Vast Wonderland West of the Missouri River, *1887.*

orange seedlings from Mission San Gabriel, he planted a two-acre orchard next to his vineyard and other crops. Wolfskill steadily acquired more land and planted more oranges, and soon his grove covered more than seventy acres. While some at the time derided the idea that oranges could be grown for profit, there being such a small population in southern California, Wolfskill recognized the market that the Gold Rush was creating, and he profited greatly by shipping his crop north to the gold fields and the burgeoning city of San Francisco. He'd become the first commercial California orange grower and, by extension, the founder of the California orange industry. An article in the *Orange Grower's Union* noted that Wolfskill "had more to do with stimulating orange growing in Southern California from that time forward than any other influence." Over the course of his life, William Wolfskill would own tens-of-thousands of acres in California, and by 1864 he was the second-highest taxpayer in what had become Los Angeles County.[15]

The next phase of the orange's march toward economic dominance was jump-started by the completion of the transcontinental railroads. The Southern Pacific punched through in 1876, and just a year later, William Wolfskill's son Joseph arranged for the first carload of California oranges to be shipped to Eastern markets. It took almost a month to get to St. Louis, but the fruit arrived in remarkably good shape. The pump was primed. A decade later, two thousand railcars of citrus were moving east annually—double that just five years later. And this was when the orange was still considered a luxury, affordable only to the wealthy. The first ventilated freight car appeared in 1887, and two years later the ice bunker car; these technologies reduced decay

Destiny—The Orange in California

LEFT: *The first commercial orange grove in California was planted by William Wolfskill in 1841 on land that later became the Southern Pacific Railroad's Arcade Depot at 5th and Alameda Streets in present-day downtown Los Angeles.*

BOTTOM: *The Wolfskill groves were a tourist showplace and profitable, but oranges in the 1860s were only "one of many promising specialty crops" being experimented with for commercial potential.*[16]

At the time I located on my place in the East San Bernardino Valley, orange culture was hardly thought of . . . . (When) I set out my grove, in 1869, I had . . . decided to take only enough to set out 1¾ acres . . . This orchard is now over twenty years old and it is believed that there is not a finer grove in California.[17]

Lewis Cram
San Bernardino Guardian, 1874

and further increased rail shipping of California's rising, new crop.

Another factor fueling the development of citriculture was the discovery that the mountains surrounding the Southern California basin create a perfect environment for growing certain orange varieties. The mountains are positioned above the coastal fog belt with mild climate and benefit from a gravelly soil made rich by millions of years of deposited sediment. Once irrigation brought water, these areas soon drew increasing numbers of serious growers. While oranges would flourish throughout much of California, the ribbon of foothills along the base of the San Gabriel and San Bernardino Mountains would become the famed "Orange Belt."

This 1905 stereocard image is labeled "Southern Pacific Train, one-half mile long, loaded with California Oranges for the East."

Destiny—The Orange in California

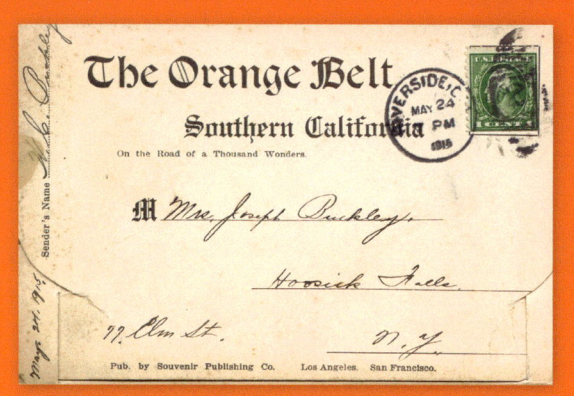

This souvenir, mailed on May 24, 1915, from Riverside, California, to Hoosick Falls, New York, contains twenty-two pictures of life among the oranges including stunning panoramas, lavish homes and flowered irrigation canals. Not shown is anyone working.

For more than a half century the citrus industry was at the center of Southern California's growth. By 1920, with annual revenues of sixty million dollars, the California orange crop trailed only oil as the golden state's largest revenue producer.

36

The Orange and the Dream of California

SWEET DREAMS ARE MADE OF THIS— JEFFERSONIAN DEMOCRACY, GERMAN SOCIAL THEORY, UTOPIAN IDEALS, AGRICULTURAL CAPITALISM, A QUEST FOR HEALTH . . . AND THE CALIFORNIA ORANGE

Thomas Jefferson believed that "those who labor in the earth are the chosen people of God, if He ever had a chosen people." Jefferson felt that citizens as "yeoman farmers," who prospered from agriculture and held a strong sense of civic duty would create the best chance for a free and democratic society.

A hundred years later, the revolutionary German lawyer, historian, sociologist, and political economist

Sent from California to someone in "Indian territory" in 1908, this postcard captures what Kevin Starr described as the "bourgeois utopia" phase of California development, when "the dream attached itself to agriculture."[18]

Destiny—The Orange in California

Orange Groves at Highland, Cal.

California was portrayed as a place where someone might reinvent themselves as a rancher, or better yet as a horticulturist, and live a civilized rural life, "self-supporting, living amidst beauty, having the means to enjoy the amenities."[19] A 1926 travel brochure for the Santa Ana Valley, east of Los Angeles in Orange County, proclaimed that "in no other place in America can one find such a thoroughly delightful combination of the best features of urban and rural life . . . Even the most remote ranch is equipped with electricity, water, gas and other city necessities."

Max Weber published *The Protestant Ethic and the Spirit of Capitalism*, in which he postulated that Protestantism influenced the development of capitalism because the Reformation redefined even routine and everyday occupations as "blessed by God" when they added to the common good. Rather than the Eastern or early Christian idea of withdrawing from the world as an aesthete, Protestantism favored engagement to conquer and change the world. Weber argued that this thinking was part of what pushed the West to forge an industrialized economy and develop capitalism.

From its earliest days of colonization, sentiments like these fueled a number of periods in America when utopian movements ebbed and flowed and attempts to fashion perfect societies were tried. The mid-nineteenth century was one of these periods. The lofty and esoteric

> *There has been created a land . . . where there are so many blandishments and other enticements of climate and of healthfulness and soil that it has become known throughout the remotest part of the United States as the gem spot of the world.*[20]
> MAJOR BEN C. TRUMAN, 1900

thoughts of Jefferson and Weber would have been understood and embraced by the wealthy former industrialists, bankers, successful entrepreneurs, and those seeking restorative health who moved to California in its early boom years. Small religious groups, temperance followers, those fighting for suffrage or an end to slavery, along with many believing in less lofty pursuits like spiritualism, were drawn to California with its promises of plenty, perfect weather and the opportunity to build something new and better.

The city of Riverside—for several decades at the end of the nineteenth and start of the twentieth century—was the crown jewel of California citriculture, a place defined by idealized living. In 1870, lawyer, activist, abolitionist, and entrepreneur Judge John W. North gathered a group of investors and bought barren former rancho land along the Santa Ana river, about sixty miles east of Los Angeles. He laid out a grid of streets and established the Riverside Colony. North then used his extensive business and political connections to entice successful, affluent, purposeful mid-westerners to move to California and begin new lives, build a community that reflected their progressive ideals, and become not farmers but horticulturalists, dedicated to improving society by providing a healthy product. In a broadside titled "A Colony for California," North proclaimed, "We invite the earnest cooperation of all good people, who wish for homes in that land . . . fit for the abode of Angels."[21]

Charles Fletcher Lummis describes this period as "the least heroic migration in history, but the most judicious; the least impulsive but the most reasonable . . . In fact they were, by and large, by far the most comfortable immigrants, financially, in history . . . Instead of by Shank's Mare, or prairie schooner, or reeking steerage, they came on palatial trains; instead of cabins, they put up beautiful homes; instead of gophering for gold, they planted gold—and it came up in ten-fold harvest."[22] Less the "naïve, dreamy idealists" of Jefferson's vision, this wave of California settlers brought "needed capital, commercial habits, and business ability."[23] By 1895, Riverside had the highest per-capita income in the United States.

Many of these newly minted California orchardists knew very little about agriculture. Their previous success had been in business, manufacturing, and the law. This inexperience became an asset that encouraged them to embrace new ideas and experimentation when confronted with challenges in irrigation, soil, picking, packing, shipping, marketing, and, perhaps most importantly, cooperation. These agricultural entrepreneurs brought confidence and a sense of moral purpose to their new endeavor as horticulturalists, believing, as David Vaught observed in the 1999 *Cultivating California: Growers, Specialty Crops, and Labor, 1875-1920*, "they were cultivating not only specialty crops, but California itself. Their mission was to promote small, virtuous communities and economic development."

San Francisco Chronicle, March 20, 1915

*I should like to rise and go
Where the golden apples grow*
Robert Louis Stevenson
"Travel," *A Child's Garden of Verses*, 1885

Citrus acreage in California grew from three thousand in 1880, to more than forty thousand in 1893. By 1915, the industry represented a two-hundred-million-dollar investment, and California citrus growers earned four times the per-capita income of the average American. Pictured here, the Case and Tallmadge families of Redlands, California, personify what McWilliams characterized as the "wealth, enterprise, and culture" that early East Coast immigrants brought to California, along with their dreams.

Destiny—the Orange in California

Among all the varieties none meets with greater favor than the navel.
Its introduction is like a romance.
San Bernardino and Riverside Counties: with Selected Biography of Actors and Witnesses, 1922

THE BIG BANG—THE BIG ORANGE: THE REMARKABLE STORY OF THE WASHINGTON NAVEL ORANGE

For the first hundred years of the orange cultivation, all California orange orchards were little more than seedling trees. Many were still the siblings of those very first trees nurtured at the missions, but by the 1870s California nurserymen were introducing budded varieties from Mexico, South America, Southern Europe, Australia, China, Japan—even England. Of the hundreds tried, only a few were found to have any real value over the "native" trees. That would change dramatically.

Seedless, or almost seedless, navel varieties had been known around the world for centuries; a Chinese writer spoke of them in 1178 AD, and an Australian navel was grown in California in the mid-nineteenth century, but was found less than satisfactory. The introduction of what became known as the Washington navel is one of the great California stories, and it altered everything—the citriculture, the economy, the environment, the population, the future.

It might never have happened if not for a remarkable woman named Eliza Tibbets, who embodied much of what California promised and became. She was curious and a free thinker; she was both of her time and ahead of her time; she was committed to her ideals and full of contradictions; she was a doer and doing her best just to get by. Born to a Cincinnati family of progressive Republican abolitionists, Eliza married three times and divorced twice, adopted an African-American child, lived in New York City where she was a practicing spiritualist, marched with Fredrick Douglas in 1871 to

THE FAMOUS CALIFORNIA NAVEL ORANGE

For centuries, growers noticed that orange trees would occasionally, spontaneously produce individual fruit different from the rest of the tree, with fewer or more seeds, a thicker or thinner skin, a sweeter or more-sour taste. One such variety, the Selecta, was cultivated in Goa and Portugal and later transplanted to the Portuguese colony, Brazil. It was from this variety that the Washington navel evolved.

The Orange and the Dream of California

> *The orange is an immigrant into the United States.*
> *Like many immigrants it has risen to fame and fortune.*
>
> CHARLES WILSON
> "Oranges—Our Golden Wealth,"
> *Nature Magazine: An Illustrated Monthly with Popular Articles about Nature*, 1924

petition for women's right to vote, and attempted with her third husband, Luther, to establish an integrated, egalitarian community in post-Civil War Virginia. All this before moving to California

Eliza and Luther were among the early Riverside émigrés. Unlike many of the others, they were not wealthy but they shared with them a vision of creating a new life for themselves, along with a better world. When they had previously lived in Washington, D.C., Eliza and Luther had known William O. Saunders, superintendent of gardens and grounds for the United States Department of Agriculture. It was undetermined what crops would sustain the newly established Riverside Colony—many were being experimented with, including wheat, grapes, different varieties of citrus, and even silkworms. Eliza wrote to Saunders asking for suggestions.

In a stroke of luck that goes beyond serendipity, Saunders had been corresponding with a Presbyterian missionary in Brazil regarding a promising variety of orange that had been cultivated there since at least 1810. Saunders sent for some samples, budded them to robust rootstalks, and named them "Washington navels." He sent several to Eliza at her request in the early 1870s. Interestingly, he also sent trees to Florida, but the soil, water, and climate conditions weren't right, and the variety never took hold.

Eliza and Luther drove their buckboard three days and sixty-five miles from Riverside to Los Angeles to pick up the small, fragile trees. On the advice of a neighbor and knowledgeable grower, the trees were soaked for some time to hydrate them, and then planted in the Tibbets' front yard. Eliza Tibbets is said to have watered them with her dishwater. Another neighbor and grower, Sam McCoy, took a few cuttings and budded them to seedling oranges on his irrigated property. Because of his careful attention, his trees produced fruit several years

The navel orange originated from what is known as a "sport"—a spontaneous, natural mutation—that results in a new kind of fruit, one with no seeds and a tiny second orange wrapped under a "navel." Since they are seedless, navels can only be propagated by grafting them to the rootstock of another variety of citrus.

Destiny—The Orange in California

before the Tibbets trees. McCoy exhibited this new California navel orange at the January 22, 1879, Southern California Horticultural Fair. It won first prize. There was an immediate market for this new variety, and the "first bearing trees were a great curiosity to the people, who drove for miles to view them and willingly paid seventy-five cents per dozen for the privilege of picking them from the trees with their own hands."[24] The original trees had become famous, important, valuable.

The Tibbets made a comfortable living selling cuttings from their two-parent trees at a dollar a piece, reportedly earning as much as twenty thousand dollars one year, an astonishing sum in the early 1880s. They enlarged their home, were active in the community, bought an elegant carriage, and enjoyed their extended family.

But Luther, though "intelligent and a good neighbor,"[25] was constantly suing or being sued over water, land, and other issues, and when the real estate boom crashed in 1887, the Tibbets' fortunes turned, and they lost their home and property a few years later. Despite the fact that every Washington navel tree in the world is a direct descendent of the Tibbets' two trees, in an O. Henry-like twist, Eliza and Luther died penniless—Eliza in 1898 and Luther, in a county charity hospital, four years later.

Large and exceptionally juicy, ripening in winter, rich in flavor, and terrifically attractive with a deep-orange skin that was easy to peel and fruit that was easy to separate, the Washington navel was the king of oranges. By the 1904-05 growing season, 31,422 carloads of Washington navel oranges were shipped out of California. LaSalle A. Maynard, in a magazine article from the time, commented that if these had been one continuous train, it would have been "over 230 miles long, reached from New York . . . to Boston with six miles to spare." The second California gold rush had begun.

Described by her biographer as "bright, alert, vivacious—full of charming personality," Eliza Tibbets moved to California in the 1870s as part of a wave of idealistic settlers hoping to create progressive new communities. Like John Chapman, better known as "Johnny Appleseed," Eliza was brought up in the Swedenborgian or New Church, which encouraged civic engagement and actions that might improve the lives of people. And like Johnny Appleseed, Eliza played a major role in the creation of vast fruit orchards. Who says you can't mix apples and oranges?

1883 — A CARLOAD OF MAMMOTH NAVEL ORANGES FROM ⎯⎯⎯⎯⎯

Sometimes a picture really is worth a thousand words; oranges were BIG in California.

On May 7, 1903, President Theodore Roosevelt helped transplant one of the two original Tibbets navel orange trees to the front of the Mission Inn in Riverside. The tree died not long after, but lives on in the millions of Washington navel trees around the world that are its direct, identical-budded descendents.

This large brass pin celebrates Riverside's role as home of the Washington navel.

Destiny—The Orange in California

45

California Becomes a Navel Power

The importance of the "King of California Oranges" was recognized early, and extensive efforts were made to preserve the surviving original tree. Moved to a park in 1902, the lone original tree struggled to survive. Experts from the University of Riverside's Citrus Research Center and Agricultural Experiment Station repeatedly had to graft fresh rootstock and employ other exceptional methods to save it.

Officials began commemorating the tree's significance, also honoring those who had planted and nurtured the very first Washington navels.

In the 1930s, disease in Brazil wiped out the entire Washington navel variety, where the fruit had originally been discovered. In a goodwill gesture, U.S. growers sent an offspring of the Tibbets' Riverside parent navel orange to growers there, which was then used to provide cuttings that eventually replenished Brazil's orchards.

From the early 1900s to about 1930, it was possible for anyone to have the snapshots they took printed as postcards. Known as "real-photo postcards," or by the acronym "RPPC," today they offer a one-of-a-kind and personal look at worlds gone by. This RPPC shows a boy looking at the surviving original Tibbets' Washington navel orange tree, which is surrounded by an iron fencing for protection. On the back of the card is written in faded ink: "One of the first orange trees brought to California—It has been kept alive by grafting young trees into the trunk."

The Orange and the Dream of California

R-74   THE PARENT NAVEL ORANGE TREE, RIVERSIDE, CALIFORNIA

ORIGINAL TREE BROUGHT FROM BAHIA, BRAZIL, IN 1873

This postcard from the late '30s shows the same tree from a different angle. The same boulder at the right of RPPC card opposite can be seen in this card with a plaque describing the tree's history and importance.

PARENT WASHINGTON NAVEL ORANGE TREE → HISTORICAL LANDMARK STATE OF CALIFORNIA No. 20

AN ORANGE SHRINE, the parent navel tree of California, was officially marked for future generations to visit by the erection and dedication at Riverside, February 17, of this first historical landmark sign. The young ladies are just adding pulchritude to the picture.

On June 1, 1932, the California Chamber of Commerce selected the Parent Navel Orange Tree to be among the first group of California Historical Landmarks. The tree and plaque are still there, at the corner of Magnolia and Arlington Avenues in Riverside. The plaque reads:

"The navel orange industry of today has back of it a romantic story that dates to a time nearly sixty years ago, when men lost heart and laughed at a woman's efforts to save and bring to life two scrubby sickly-looking little orange plants. Had it been left to those men, the navel industry never would have been known in the southwest, the only spot in the United States to which the Navel takes kindly." This photo is from the March 1933 issue of California Highways and Public Works.

Destiny—the Orange in California

47

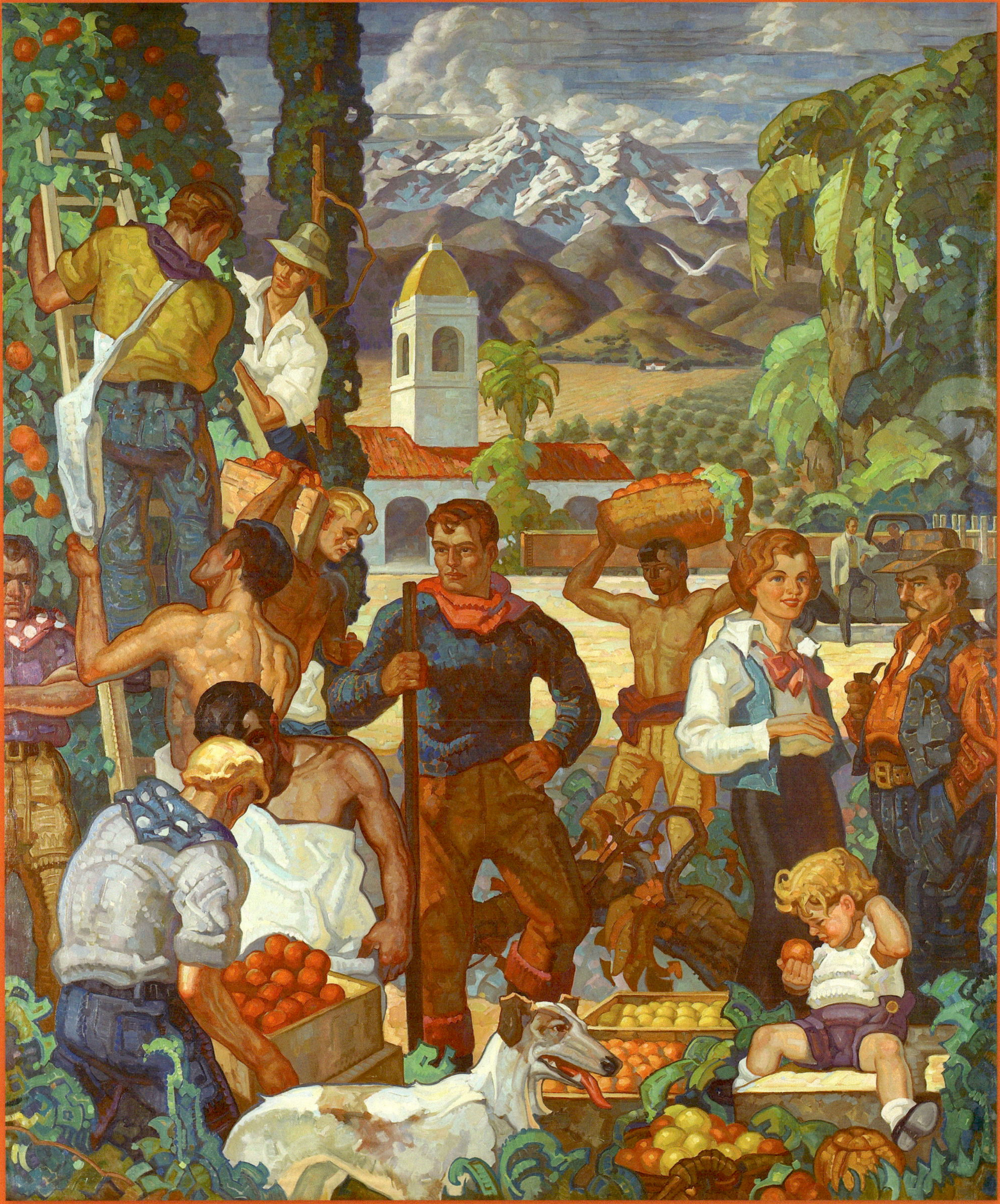

California's Real Gold Rush— The Sunkist Story

Even Paradise requires promoters, marketing salesmen to herald not only its ethereal splendors, but also its mundane perks.
TIMOTHY WHITE
The Nearest Faraway Place: Brian Wilson, the Beach Boys, and the Southern California Experience, 1994

Railroads and new markets, expanding orchards and the navel orange; the romance and dream were spreading across the country. But in California, growing oranges meant hard work and uncertainty. Orange growers were going broke.

Regional consumers were still the primary market for California oranges well into the early 1890s. The orange was still exotic in much of the country; most Americans had never seen one. Expensive, oranges came individually wrapped in tissue paper—to help reduce spoilage in shipping—which only increased their reputation as a luxury item. Even with an increasing number of railroads expanding the opportunities for shipping oranges to the populated East, ever-growing production outpaced demand.

During this period, shipping agents visited groves, estimated the value of fruit on the tree, and paid the grower. The fruit—picking, packing, shipping,

OPPOSITE: *A series of large-scale murals were created for the boardroom of the Art Deco-inspired Sunkist building built in 1935. Painted by Frank Bowers and Arthur Prunier, the works depict an idealized history of the orange in California. The murals survive and are today in Sunkist's Southern California headquarters.*

Formed in troublous times, in an attempt to bring a semblance of order out of the chaos of overproduction, distant markets and consumer apathy...

STUART O. BLYTHE
California—Magazine of Pacific Business, 1937

selling—was then the agent's responsibility. This worked for a while, but the agents had no control over what happened once the fruit arrived at its destination: how much was selling, in which cities, what types were most popular, how much had spoiled.

In the early 1890s, agents changed their policy and began only handling fruit on consignment. All the risk became the growers. Now in addition to their responsibilities of planting, irrigating, controlling disease, and frost protection, they were also in charge of getting their product to consumers. Owners of any-sized orchard were forced to accept whatever was offered by local speculators or consign their fruit to East Coast commission men. Distribution was open to manipulation, exploitation, and dishonesty; brokers "might sell a grower's oranges at a low price in the morning and then have an accomplice resell them at a high price by nightfall."[26] For the California orange grower, "ruin stared him in the face."[27] The national Great Depression of 1893 added to their woes. These became known as the "red-ink years."

California orange growers with previous business

What was to become one of the most recognized brands in the world, Sunkist, began at a meeting of beleaguered California orange growers on the second floor of the Mott Building in Los Angeles to discuss their collective worries and challenges.

The Orange and the Dream of California

While the idea of bohemian gentility through citriculture was being promoted and promised, on the ground it was challenges, uncertainty and constant work.

experience began to look for solutions. As early as 1885, groups of growers attempted to organize and find ways to manage their challenges. The Claremont Fruit Growers Association and Riverside's Pachappa Orange Growers Association were two successful early groups that collectively packed and shipped their oranges directly to the East. Several prominent growers noticed these groups' success, and on April 4, 1893, organized a meeting of about a hundred other concerned orchardists on the second floor of a building at Main and Second streets in Los Angeles, just a handful of blocks from where William Wolfskill had established the very first commercial California orange orchard only a half-century before.

After vigorous discussion, the group agreed to organize along the lines of the previously successful but much smaller cooperatives, pooling their fruit, concentrating on quality, and sharing the expenses of packing and marketing. A five-person committee was formed to devise the details and establish the logistics.. Remarkably, only one member of this group was an orange grower by profession. The others—while all active and successful growers—had made their original marks as doctors or lawyers.

By the fall of 1893 the new cooperative organization, the Southern California Fruit Growers Exchange, was up and running, immediately successful in providing its members control and stability over their production and distribution. Not all growers joined—there was severe pushback from entrenched interests—and competitors formed a number of other cooperative organizations, but the California Fruit Growers Exchange, as the organization was renamed in 1895 when northern California growers joined, had the vision, the knowledge, and the willingness to seek experts and try new approaches. They soon became the center of California's citrus industry. In doing so, this cooperative organization changed almost everything about the orange in California, California itself and, in a number of significant ways, the country as a whole.

In 1908, the Exchange's Chicago-based, pioneering advertising agency, Lord and Thomas, coined a name to use in ad campaigns. A few months later this name was adopted for use on the Exchange's highest-quality oranges. The name? Sunkist, and with that the California orange was now a brand.

California's Real Gold Rush—The Sunkist Story

The people are more anxious to cooperate, and appreciate scientific experiments more, than any other class that I have met.

G. Harold Powell, U.S. Department of Agriculture pomologist
Letter from California commenting on California orange growers, 1904

Left: *The first Sunkist logo.* Right: *In the era of handset type, brass dies like this one were supplied by Sunkist to newspapers to be used in ads produced for local grocers.*

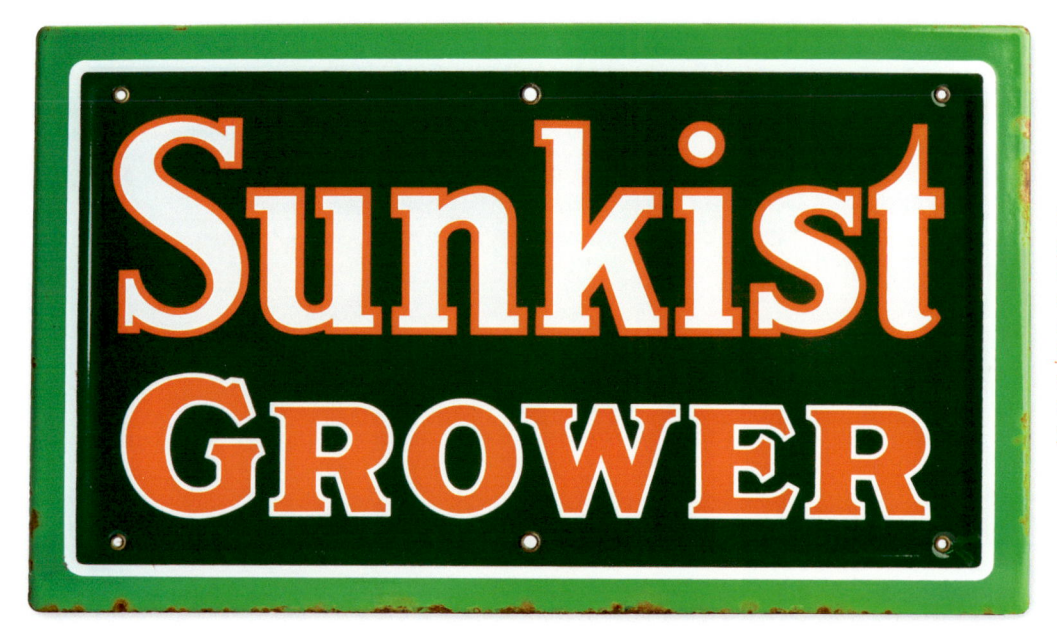

The Sunkist name was promoted even in the groves. High-quality porcelain signs—eighteen inches long—were available from the Exchange for $1.45. Custom versions were available that included the grower's name and packinghouse.

52   The Orange and the Dream of California

10,500 Growers

203 Local Associations

20 District Exchanges

CALIFORNIA FRUIT GROWERS' EXCHANGE

850 Car-Lot Markets
63 Districts

2,500 Jobbers

400,000 Retailers

113,000,000 Consumers (U·S· & Canada)

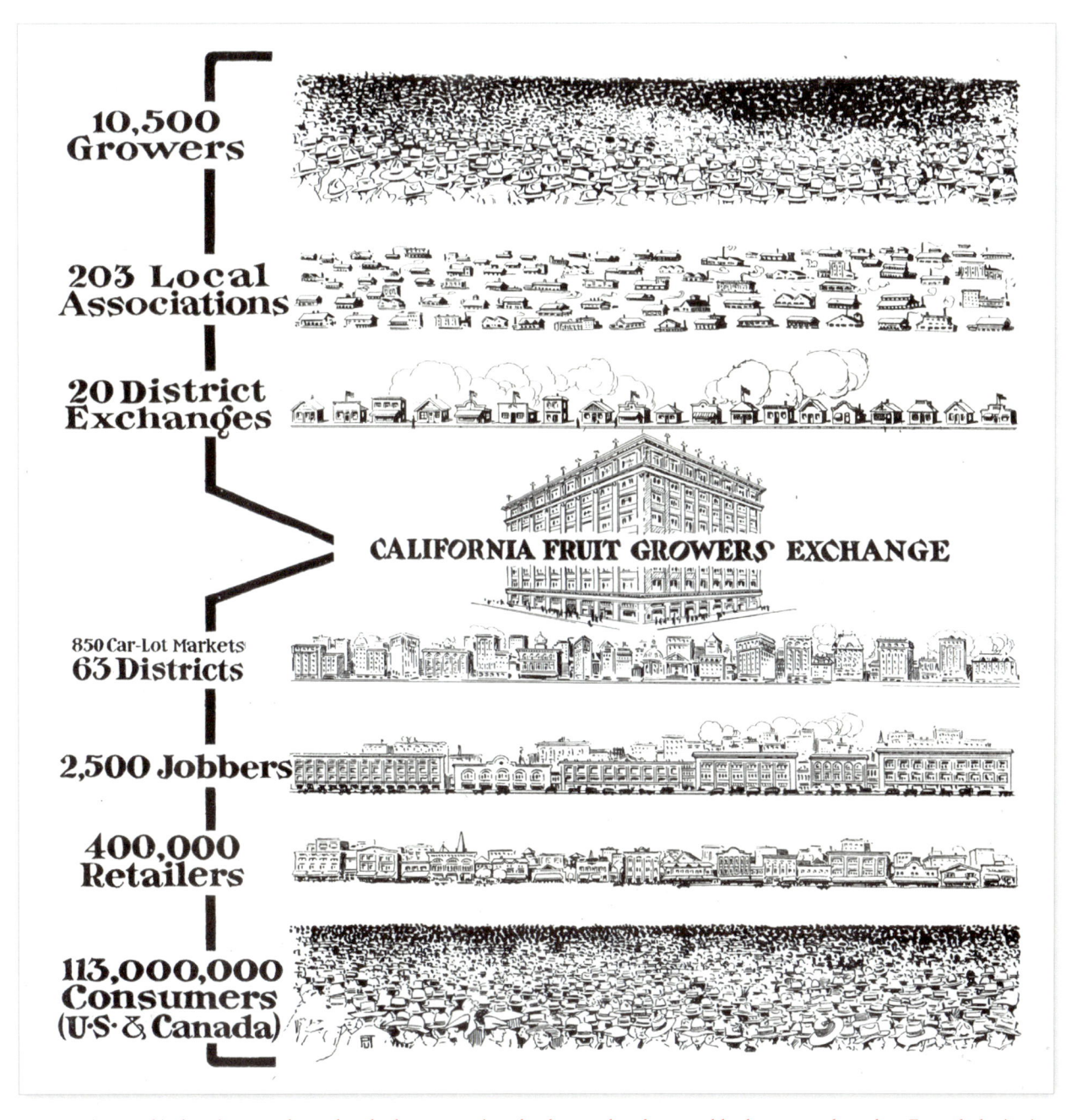

As a cooperative, Sunkist has, for more than a hundred years, continued to be owned and operated by the growers themselves. From the beginning, management was made up of growers who are elected by members to govern the organization. With input from staff and much encouragement from its advertising agency, the California Fruit Growers Exchange created and implemented a remarkable number of innovative processes, programs, and products that changed the way the country thought about the orange. This chart is from a 1922 pamphlet promoting Sunkist to grocers.

California's Real Gold Rush—The Sunkist Story

There is plenty of hard work about orange growing . . .
Not only work, but money and patience are required . . .
So much depends on the manner in which they are cultivated and cared for.
Land of Sunshine, July 1894

First Things First—Perfecting the Basics

Getting healthy, attractive fruit to faraway consumers was an enormous challenge. The trip East took weeks and, even with refrigerated railcars, there were sometimes losses of as much as twenty-five percent. Typically, the members of the California Fruit Growers Exchange looked to science, technology, and experts for answers. Influential growers used their contacts to petition the U.S. Department of Agriculture for help, arguing that federal assistance was warranted because the problem was interstate-related.

The USDA sent G. Harold Powell, who was the pomologist [a botanist specializing in the study of fruit] in charge of fruit storage and transportation investigations. After bustling "about the California southland with itinerant mania, conferring with his team, visiting orchards and packinghouses, meeting with growers and packers, bankers and businessmen, marketers and machinists,"[28] Powell provided convincing evidence that, as he wrote in a 1904 letter, "the growers themselves were the primary cause of decay." Powell's recommendations were simple and inexpensive to implement, yet they collectively made a dramatic difference. Among them: having pickers wear gloves; using specially designed clippers with blunt ends to prevent nicks; keeping boxes of picked fruit in the shade to stay cool until they were hauled to the packinghouse; and a variety of other common sense ways to reduce orange bruising during packing. Sunkist growers readily adopted all of Powell's suggestions.

The use of refrigerated railcars to ship citrus began in 1889, with ice replaced along the way.

What Makes Harold Run—
A Guy on the Go, Growing an Industry

While Sunkist was established as a cooperative of growers run by its members, they were savvy enough to find and incorporate a number of brilliant, non-grower individuals to help guide them. G. Harold Powell is the archetype of the east coast, well-educated, hard driving, idealist-and-opportunist who made Sunkist into an economic powerhouse. Contemporaries and biographers gush about him:

"... family man, a laboratory and field scientist, a highly skilled manager of people, a humanist with appreciation for the arts, and a captivating dinner table conversationalist ... "
Richard Lillard, editor *Letters from the Orange Empire*

"... a schmooze artist of prodigious charisma and had a brain the size of Milwaukee ... "
Delores Hanney, *Sun Kissed*

"He was a born diplomat. He had a wonderful ability to sift and analyze any question and, brushing aside superficial things, arrive at a right conclusion."
C.C. Teague, G. Harold Powell Memorial, 1922

Powell was born in Ghent, New York, in 1872, into a family that traced its roots back to the Mayflower. He graduated from Cornell with a master's degree in agriculture and was soon rising up the ladder at the U.S. Department of Agriculture. After his assignment assessing the spoilage challenges of California orange growers, he was invited to make his report at the 1908 International Refrigeration Congress at the Sorbonne in Paris, where he headed the American delegation.

In 1911, he joined the California Fruit Growers Exchange. He soon became its general manager. Powell guided Sunkist through its most dynamic, influential era, when the orange was second-only to oil in California when it came to revenue.

Powell was "considered the most influential man in Southern California" in 1922, and on February 18, while being toasted, was called "the future senator from California." Powell answered, "I'll have to think about that," leaned forward and died. He was fifty.[29]

A few weeks before, he wrote: "The measure of a man is not to be taken by his material accomplishments, but by what he makes of himself; by his self-realization, his knowledge of life's purposes and his harmonious adjustment to its expressions." Such sentiments perfectly reflect the high-mindedness and entrepreneurialism that drove those who established the California citrus industry and made Sunkist the best known brand of fresh fruit in the world.

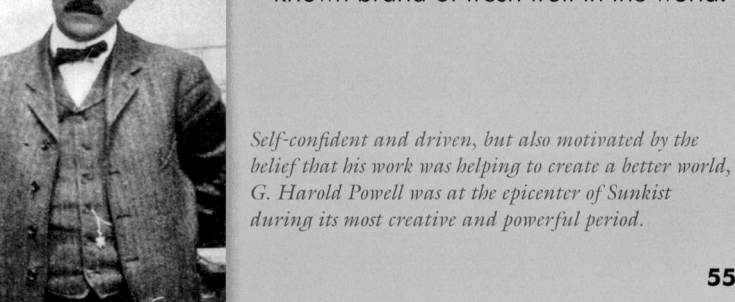

Self-confident and driven, but also motivated by the belief that his work was helping to create a better world, G. Harold Powell was at the epicenter of Sunkist during its most creative and powerful period.

California's Real Gold Rush—The Sunkist Story

Start Spreadin' the News—Sunkist Advertising

Before the California Fruit Growers Exchange and Sunkist, perishable fresh fruit had never been nationally advertised. While some growers were reluctant to invest in advertising, the Exchange, as usual, was eager to seek growth through imaginative, bold actions. In 1908, working cooperatively with the Southern Pacific Railroad, who matched the Exchange's contribution of ten thousand dollars, a train carrying exclusively California oranges was sent to Iowa. The train was decorated with banners that blared "Oranges for Health—California for Wealth." Three-color ads—almost unheard-of-at-the-time—were run in Iowa newspapers. Copy declared "Orange Week" and offered consumers multiple reasons to buy oranges: "the healthful lunch should include an orange," "California oranges are highly recommended by physicians as an aid to good health," and all the stores were having "special sales." But even with numerous practical reasons to enjoy an orange, the ad also promoted the idea that the California orange was California, a place that you'd like to visit, to experience, to live.

That year, national citrus sales increased by seventeen percent, but in Iowa, where the advertising blitz took place, sales of oranges increased fifty percent. The growers of the Exchange were convinced. Budgets increased steadily, and Sunkist became an innovator in the developing art and science of advertising. All of the themes expressed in the very first ad—extraordinary taste, good health, smart parenting, natural purity and real value—would be repeated and refined many times in Sunkist ads over the decades.

"From California the year 'round" proclaims this Sunkist billboard. Sunkist began stamping its name on every one of its oranges beginning in 1926. This sign advertises "Each orange trademarked for your protection!"

The Orange and the Dream of California

The California Fruit Growers Exchange and Southern Pacific Railroad partnered on an integrated marketing campaign that featured special events, public relations, in-store displays and full-page, color newspaper ads. Sales jumped fifty percent. The first California citrus ad featured a cartoon by Jay Norward "Ding" Darling. Darling later won two Pulitzer Prizes for his political cartoons and headed the U.S. Biology Survey, forerunner of the U.S. Fish and Wildlife Service.

California's Real Gold Rush—The Sunkist Story

You never saw an orange with a worm in it.
—Don Francisco

Before *Mad Men*, There Was Don Francisco

Born in Michigan in 1891, he joined the Chicago office of the California Fruit Growers Exchange as a fruit inspector in 1914. He soon became an assistant advertising manager and later moved to Lord and Thomas, one of the industry's pioneering agencies, where he was named executive vice president and general manager of its Los Angeles office. He oversaw the Sunkist account until the beginning of World War II.

In a 1955 speech looking back on his career, he said, "At the beginning an orange seemed to be just an orange. Everybody knew all there was to know about it. It was good to eat, of course, but had no other value."

Francisco changed all that.

In a small notebook, he jotted down ideas as they came to him. At a time when oranges were luxuries, he came up with the "Drink an Orange" campaign, and consumption of oranges increased more than six times as fast as the population. Observing that "breakfast is a habit meal," he promoted oranges for breakfast. Sales rose. In an era when the benefits of vitamins were often in the news, his Sunkist ads quoted scientific findings regarding the vitamins in oranges. "The habit of drinking orange juice was deliberately and painstakingly developed and created through advertising and promotion," he said.

Francisco believed that selling California helped sell California oranges. "We introduced certain things in the illustrations that Florida didn't have. We showed pretty girls picking oranges against a background of California missions, snow peaks and orange groves." Consumers wrote in asking for copies of the art used in this advertising, and Sunkist sold thousands of reproductions to people who framed them as art and hung them in their homes.

In the early decades of the twentieth century the advertising industry was maturing, incorporating research, new findings in psychology, embracing the burgeoning of mass media, and integrating its channels of communication. Don Francisco was one of the architects of modern advertising, who captained Sunkist's marketing during its most dynamic era.

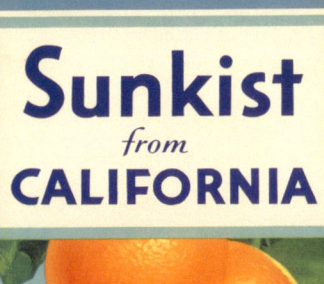

California's Real Gold Rush—The Sunkist Story 59

The Fruit of a Hundred Uses

Who knows another that is so delicious, so beneficial, or so easy to serve daily in so many tempting ways?

From California's sun-kissed groves; from soil that only California offers; from Nature's finest orange trees, cared for by the world's most expert growers, come these delicious, rich, full-flavored

California Sunkist Oranges

Famous Seedless Navels

Sweet, firm, tender—filled with golden juice. What other fruit tastes like it? What other is so good, or good for you?

Give the children oranges—at every meal, between meals, and at bedtime. Serve them on the table daily—a hundred dishes offer new delights almost without end.

Oranges cost little. But oranges—merely because they keep you well—would be economical.

A beautiful *free book*, handsomely printed in colors, entitled, "Sunkist Salads and Desserts," will be sent to any housewife who asks for it. Just send the coupon.

Full-ripened Sunkist Oranges are picked daily, *the year 'round*, in California and shipped to every market by fast freight. Thus you may depend on *freshness, quality* and *flavor*.

California Seedless Sunkist Navel Oranges always peel freely. The tissue-thin walls that enclose the sections permit easy separation without the loss of juice—you may eat these oranges whole conveniently; you may slice them *wafer*-thin for salads and desserts. Sunkists are never tough.

Order California Sunkist Oranges today. *Buy them by the box. Insist on "Sunkist"!*

Why We Make This Offer of Handsome Sunkist Premiums

The color of Sunkist fruits is so beautiful that dealers like to take the wrappers off to show it. To induce them to allow these wrappers to remain—to be sure that you get Sunkist—we offer beautiful premiums in exchange for Sunkist wrappers. So, in buying, ask the dealer for the *wrapped* fruit. Then send 12 wrappers from Sunkist Oranges or Lemons with 12 cents (24 wrappers and 24 cents if you want two spoons, etc.) and get a genuine Wm. Rogers & Son tea spoon, or orange spoon of same design. There is, of course, no advertising on these pieces. Start a set of this design. We guarantee this silver, and refund your money if not satisfactory in every way.

Mail the Coupon

Send the coupon now for the book, "Sunkist Salads and Desserts." It describes the many Sunkist uses and tells just how to get the full set of genuine Rogers Silverware, which includes 46 beautiful and useful pieces.

California Fruit Growers Exchange
Dept. A3—139 North Clark Street, Chicago

Send me the book, "Sunkist Salads and Desserts," describing the many Sunkist uses and telling how to get any or all of the 46 Sunkist premiums in exchange for Sunkist Orange or Lemon wrappers.

Name

Street

City   State

Sunkist Lemons

The best lemons to serve with fish and meats, or in tea and lemonade, are Sunkist. The skin has a clear, bright lemon color, so these lemons are the most appetizing in appearance. They slice like Sunkist Oranges. Practically seedless—full-flavored, tart and juicy. Serve them once on your table, use them once in your kitchen—you'll always buy Sunkist.

Every first-class dealer handles Sunkist Oranges and Lemons

Changing the World, One Orange at a Time—Sunkist's Big Ideas

Turning Gold into Silver—How Tissue Paper Changed America's Dining Table

The success of making Sunkist synonymous in consumers' minds with the highest quality created a new challenge. Some grocers removed the tissue wrappers printed with the Sunkist name that covered every Sunkist orange. To give the tissue wrappers value, encourage customers to ask for Sunkist fruit, and to make sure that dealers kept the wrappers on the oranges, Sunkist developed a premium program: by sending in twelve wrappers and twelve cents, a customer would be sent a silver plated spoon. The spoon was narrow, pointed—specially designed for eating oranges—and featured an orange and orange blossoms on the handle. Sunkist was soon flooded with orders for spoons—a "staggering total of over five thousand a day."[30] Customers began requesting other pieces, and the Exchange responded by offering knives, forks and serving pieces so that people could eventually collect a complete dining set. Many a newlywed couple set up housekeeping with Sunkist flatware. The California Fruit Growers Exchange/Sunkist became the single largest purchaser of silverware in the world, buying a million pieces a year between 1912 and 1917.

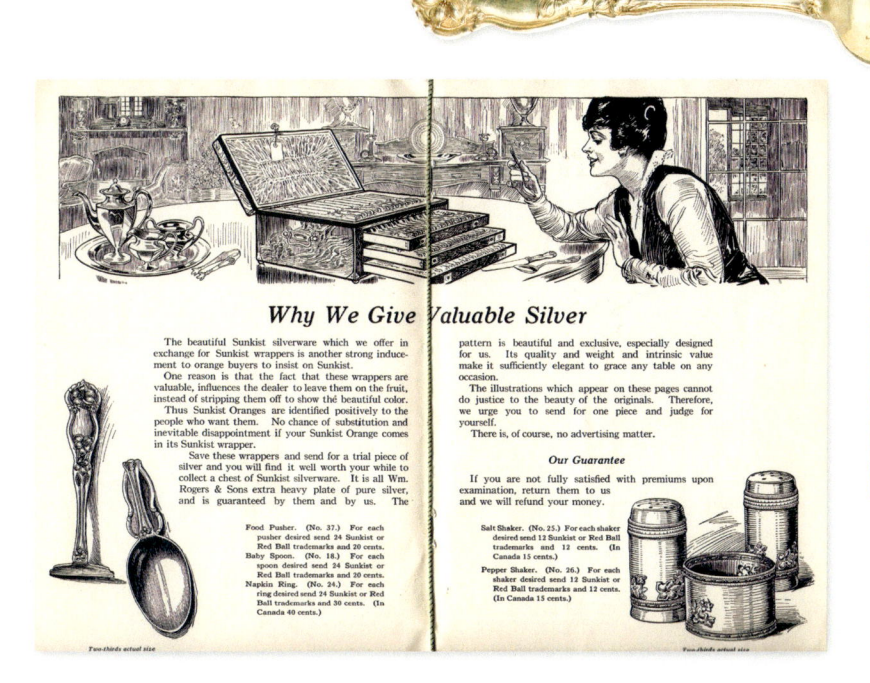

California's Real Gold Rush—The Sunkist Story

Big juicy oranges ... that carry to you the breath of the tropics, the wholesomeness of blended sun and sky and the healing, stimulating purity of sea air and mountain breezes.
1908 newspaper ad promoting California oranges

Oranges Aren't Just for Eating Anymore—Nature's Products for Industry

There are, as Pierre Laszlo noted in his 2007 book *Citrus: A History,* hidden "treasures within citrus." In another program capitalizing on the orange as more than "just an orange," the California Fruit Growers Exchange set up a separate division in 1918 to mine the oils and chemicals in citrus peel and pulp. Known as the Exchange Orange Products Company, it found new gold in developing products used in drink flavorings, pharmaceuticals, perfume, food seasonings, and other industrial needs made from oranges and lemons discarded as unfit for consumption.

BOTTOM LEFT: *The Exchange Orange Products Company facility in 1926, Ontario, California.*
CENTER: *The label reads: "Crushed in California from Tree Ripe Fruit."*
RIGHT: *All of these products, whether natural or artificial, stressed that they were made from California oranges.*

The Orange and the Dream of California

*One . . . advantage California oranges enjoyed was their color.
It's pretty obvious, but we hadn't fully realized it. We had demonstrations
of what mass displays of golden oranges would do in a dealer's window.*

Don Francisco
Executive Vice President and General Manager
Lord and Thomas, Sunkist's advertising agency

Sweet Smell of Success—Selling California at the Corner Grocery Store

The Exchange sold oranges in railroad car lots. No one knew what happened to the fruit after the car was unloaded. So beginning in 1904, the Exchange built an extensive, national organization of regional representatives. These "dealer service men" made visits to thousands of grocer retailers in big cities and small towns, demonstrating attractive ways to display fruit and calibrate costs and pricing. They worked with store owners to reduce spoilage, increase profits, improve margins, and keep prices competitive. Studying effective fruit-selling methods wherever they went, these Sunkist field representatives shared the lessons they learned in illustrated booklets given free to stores. In an era before supermarkets, people shopped in corner grocery stores, and Sunkist pioneered the use of providing retailers with colorful, attractive display materials celebrating the Sunkist name. While the displays communicated recurring messages of superior taste, freshness, and the promise of good health, they also reinforced the idea that Sunkist oranges came from that sunny, beautiful place called California.

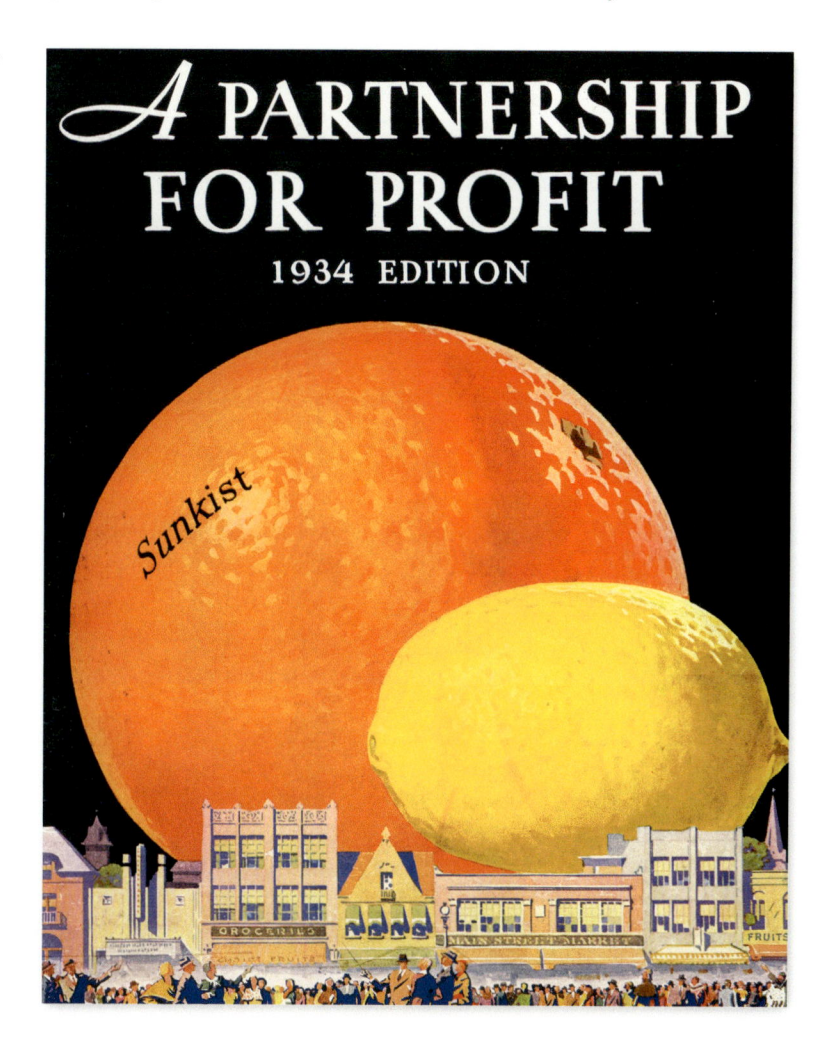

California's Real Gold Rush—The Sunkist Story

"Succeed with Sunkist. Put display—your star salesman—to work in your store and check the results" advised a 1931 booklet, published at the depth of the Depression. It showed floor plans, window displays, and the enormous variety of marketing and promotional materials available to grocers from Sunkist. This magazine ad, while aimed at consumers, promoted grocers stocking Sunkist; it promised "All first-class retailers are now offering abundant supplies of Sunkist uniformly good oranges."

Your Grocer
—How He is Serving You

MILLIONS of people—perhaps you—could not have fresh fruits and vegetables daily were it not for the three hundred thousand retailers who help assemble and distribute the nation's foods.

These merchants form the very vital link between you and the producer. They make it possible to secure needed perishable foods with convenience and dispatch. And that is a great service.

Except for this service tons of food would spoil and you would go without—oranges for example, which are regarded by physicians and other food authorities as of prime importance in a well-balanced diet.

Some foods may be high in price, due to a shortage. But this doesn't apply to oranges. Because of a plentiful supply oranges are obtainable at prices to suit everybody's purse. California's bumper crop must be marketed at home.

So buy a dozen today. Serve attractive, *economical* orange desserts instead of more costly kinds. Eat oranges freely. Let children have them.

In cutting down food bills remember that *health* is economy and that *fresh fruits and vegetables* are needed by every grown-up, and every little child.

All first-class retailers are now offering abundant supplies of

Sunkist
Uniformly Good Oranges

We will send free on request a valuable recipe book by Miss Alice Bradley of Miss Farmer's School of Cookery, Boston. It contains scores of suggestions for serving oranges and lemons.

California Fruit Growers Exchange. A Co-operative, Non-Profit Organization of 8000 Growers. Dept. M-96. Los Angeles, California.

"Oranges for Health"

The Orange and the Dream of California

The California Fruit Growers Exchange promoted the value of its Sunkist brand to retailers. This cartoon is from a 1922 booklet called 52 Dividends a Year–To Retail Merchants *that proudly proclaims "more than 137 million copies of magazines and newspapers . . . will contain Sunkist advertising."*

California's Real Gold Rush—The Sunkist Story

Before the Flood—The Invention of Orange Juice

There was a time when orange juice didn't exist. Well, the juice existed, of course, but outside of those who worked in citrus orchards, no one was drinking it. A hundred years ago, if a person was fortunate enough to have an orange, it was cut in half, often shared, and typically eaten with a spoon.

With California scrub brush being transformed by irrigation into thousands of new acres of orange groves; with the navel ripening in the winter and the Valencia in the summer; with great strides being made in disease control; and with the ability to quickly and safely get high-quality fruit from the tree to anywhere, supply soon surpassed demand. The energetic, clever minds at Sunkist again saw opportunity.

Launched in 1916, the "Drink an Orange" campaign promoted the *idea* of orange juice for the first time. It was another Don Francisco initiative. Sunkist magazine ads, store displays and streetcar signs showed healthy, happy babies, shiny-faced children, doting moms and confident businessmen starting their day with orange juice. Scenes of immaculate groves and snow-covered mountains were often included. The campaign exceeded all expectations, seeing serving size grow from half an orange to two to three.

The quick adoption of orange juice as a regular part of the American breakfast and diet was accelerated by two events that played out during the same period: the discovery that vitamins play an important role in good health and the global flu pandemic of 1918-19. Americans had a new awareness and interest in caring for their health. Sunkist presented California oranges as "health insurance coupled with a fantasy of a tropical paradise."[31] The California citrus industry was generating $48 million in 1917, and the California Fruit Growers Exchange represented sixty-nine percent of the state's citrus volume during this period.

Ironically, while California's Sunkist invented the popular consumption of orange juice, virtually all oranges grown for juice today are grown in Florida. Florida oranges contain lots of moisture but are inferior-looking fruit, making Florida the leader in processed juice. But as John McPhee notes, while Florida now "grows three times as many oranges . . . California oranges, for their part, can safely be called three times as beautiful." Nine of every ten oranges eaten fresh in America are grown in California.

Sunkist produced orange juice promotional materials targeted at children, women, men . . . even teenagers.
The small poster at the lower left was offered to lunch counters and soda fountains.

California's Real Gold Rush—The Sunkist Story

67

Juicy Details—the Evolution of the Orange Juicer

To enjoy orange juice, one needs a handy way to juice an orange. Once again Sunkist saw opportunity. On August 17, 1916, Don Francisco jotted in his notebook, "Arrange with some concern such as Mason Fruit Jar Company to market extractors." Soon Sunkist ads were promoting "Drink an Orange" and offering "Big, Convenient Orange Juice Extractors" at "Actual Cost." Millions were sold.

Next came electric juicers or "extractors." The Exchange contracted with the A.C. Gilbert Company, in New Haven, Connecticut, to manufacture juicers made to its specifications. The company also made fans, hair dryers, and mixers; during World War II, it produced equipment for military aircraft. Company founder Alfred Carlton Gilbert had invented the Erector Set in 1911, purchased American Flyer toy trains in 1938, and produced children's chemistry sets and microscopes. His company was for many years one of the largest toy manufacturers in the world.

Beginning in the early 1920s, Sunkist offered an evolving line of electric juicers for both home and commercial use. Fresh-squeezed orange juice competed with Coca-Cola and other soft drinks at soda fountains and drugstore lunch counters.

This 1917 ad advises readers to "drink an orange or two daily" and that "these natural ways to insure health are being advised by physicians more and more every day." Sunkist extractors were available at retail stores for ten cents, or twenty-four cents by mail.

The Orange and the Dream of California

The "Sunkist Junior" electric juicer was offered from the early 1920s to the '30s, when it was replaced by "Sunkist Juicit," which was sold for over twenty years. Both styles evolved to meet changing tastes in colors. Early versions of both came with bowls made of Jadeite.

A Sunkist electric juice extractor cost fifteen dollars in 1929, the equivalent of more than two hundred dollars today.

With sixty thousand soda fountains across the country in 1922, providing commercial-grade juicers opened up another new market for Sunkist.

California's Real Gold Rush—The Sunkist Story

Zest!—Orange Recipes to Keep Them Reaching for More

Before the orange was the stuff of legends, a symbol of California's promise, and a major economic power, it was something to eat. With compelling color, amazing fragrance, and arriving in its own perfect packaging, the orange was—and is—juicy, flavorful, healthy, and could even make other foods taste better.

As oranges became plentiful and affordable, much effort was put into encouraging Americans to incorporate them into their diet, not just as something to be peeled and eaten as a snack but as a daily part of breakfast, lunch, and dinner. The California orange—and the ability to buy and enjoy it—became an integral part of the new, expanding American middle class.

Sunkist produced many recipe booklets. Always stylishly designed and often containing dishes from top chefs, the booklets were offered free to consumers. It is likely there were few homes in America without at least one Sunkist recipe pamphlet in their kitchen cupboard.

BOTTOM LEFT: *This 1940 collection of orange recipes is one of the most colorful Sunkist produced and came in an equally beautiful envelope that was illustrated with a perfect California orange orchard.*
BOTTOM RIGHT: *Art Deco inspired, this spectacularly illustrated 1920 booklet added the sophistication and allure of New York to California's King Citrus.*

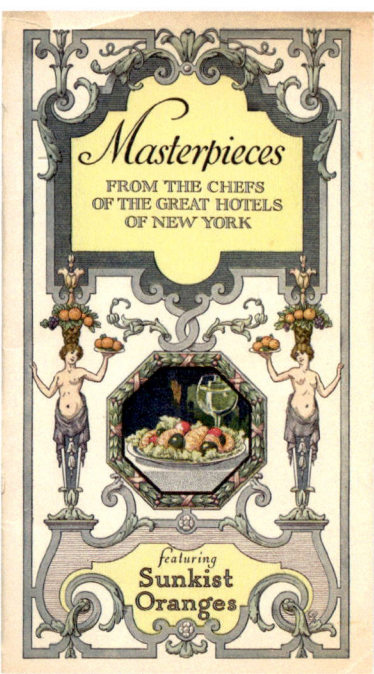

70

The Orange and the Dream of California

LEFT: *This collection of recipes came on colorful cards ready for filing.*

RIGHT: *Sunkist produced recipe booklets for years, each with a particular focus: from drinks to desserts, and from healthy eating to dishes for children.*

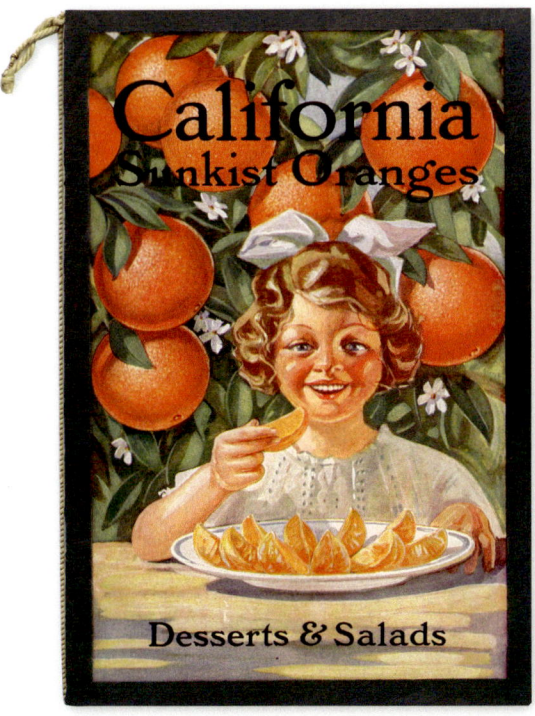

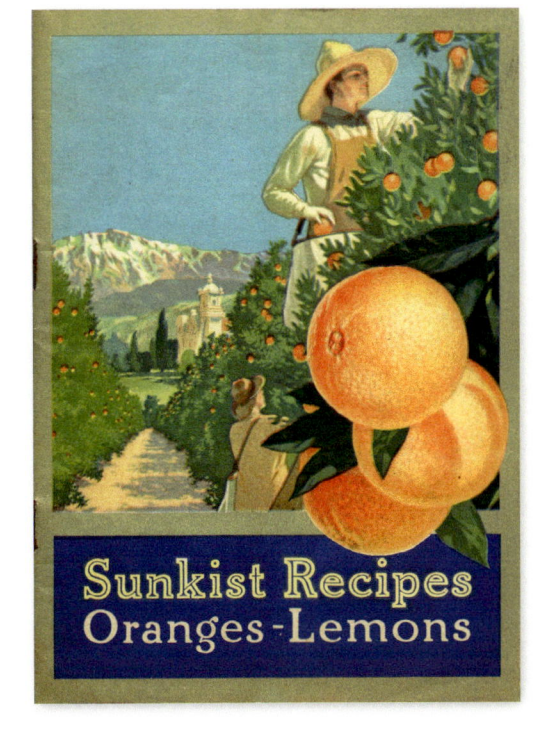

LEFT: *This early example from 1915, produced when "Orange Blossom" flatware from Sunkist was at its most popular, features— in addition to recipes— a different flatware piece from the collection on every page.*

RIGHT: *With a cover featuring an idealized image of California citrus growing, this 1916 booklet had equally attractive etchings and color illustrations inside. Many of the recipes offered here were used in later pamphlets too.*

California's Real Gold Rush—The Sunkist Story

71

"O" is for Orange— Readin', Writin' and the Orange

Sunkist began providing educational materials almost from the very beginning. The items ranged from special bulletins aimed at cooking-school classes for women, describing "the many delightful and novel methods of preparing and serving oranges and lemons," to specialized materials for teachers and students. "Right now, in the schools and colleges of the country, from the Kindergartens to the Universities, Sunkist is educating a whole new group of buyers for you," began a chapter from a 1934 booklet for retailers titled *A Partnership for Profit*.

TOP: *Sunkist proudly stated that "parents and teachers everywhere write to Sunkist for information . . . on the healthy values of Sunkist citrus fruits." The Exchange gave out more than five million pieces of educational literature in 1936.*[32]

BOTTOM: *This coloring book was produced by Sunkist and given to teachers throughout the 1930s.*

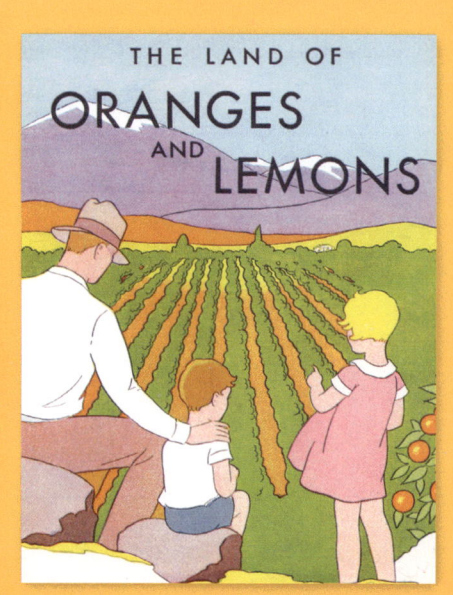

Schools, cooking classes, women's clubs, and other educational centers were furnished with Sunkist booklets and bulletins on the history, growing, health value, and recipe options of California citrus.

The Orange and the Dream of California

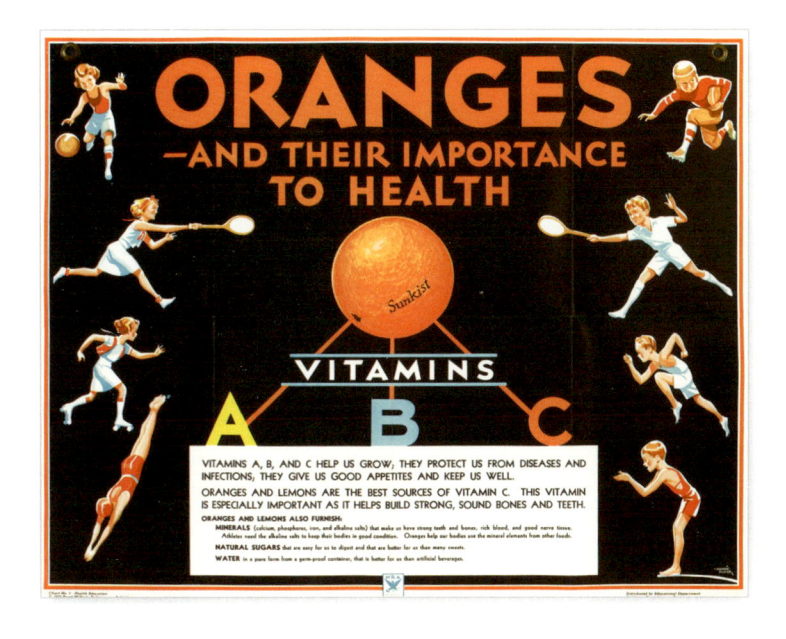

From a 1931 Sunkist booklet for retailers: "By continually developing new uses, new methods of preparing, new ideas in serving its fruits—by developing new buyers and stimulating the established markets, Sunkist advertising has proved to be the powerful factor in creating the demand for many millions of boxes of Oranges—thereby creating additional profits of millions of dollars for Sunkist merchants."

As Sunkist advertising became more "benefit" focused in the 1930s, visual representation of pristine California landscapes diminished. "We decided that all those extra features that we had in the background were really distractions," said Don Francisco, "[we didn't want people] thinking we had any interest in selling property or tourist attractions. . . . We began advertising the fruit itself." What did not change, however, was the practice of always identifying Sunkist oranges as grown in California.

In 1952, the California Fruit Growers Exchange changed its name to Sunkist Growers, Inc. It had become, McWilliams noted, "the most efficient marketing co-operative in the world" and developed Sunkist into one of the most successful trademarks in history. In doing so, Sunkist had brought structure, strength, science, and savvy to the growing, packing, shipping, and marketing of the California orange. Sunkist took something that "most Americans had never laid eyes on"[33] in the 1880s, and made it as common as California sunshine.

California's Real Gold Rush—The Sunkist Story

Chicago in the late nineteenth century was a major market for California oranges. Shipped there, they were then distributed to the rest of the United States. The 1893 Chicago World's Fair, also known as the World Columbian Exposition, was held from May to October that year in honor of the four-hundredth anniversary of Columbus' discovery of the New World. Christopher Columbus brought the seeds of oranges and other citrus to the Americas on his second voyage. The Southern Pacific Railroad brought seventy-three railroad cars of California fruits and flowers to the Columbian Exposition, enough to make these displays, have an orchard of living trees, and give away over two hundred thousand oranges on "California Day."

This tower of oranges was part of the Los Angeles County exhibit at the fair. The base was fourteen feet square and the tower, beginning with a diameter of five feet and tapering up, rose to a height of thirty-two feet. Around the tower were displayed the major varieties of oranges then grown in California: Malta Bloods, Mediterranean Sweets, Wilson Seedlings, Joppas, St. Michaels, Konahs, and Australian and Washington navels.

5

Fantasyland—
Expositions and Orange Shows

Picture yourself in a room full of wonder, with trees full of oranges and marmalade skies. That's what it was like at an orange show. The orange had been made the center of *everything*, and everything was made of oranges: animals, buildings, locomotives . . . everything. Imagine the fragrance as you walked into the hall; it would have been intoxicating.

At the other end of the Chicago Fair's Horticultural Building was this full-size replica of the Liberty Bell, complete with crack, made entirely of California oranges. The caption for this etching from a souvenir book says the display was sponsored by the city of San Diego, but the words "Los Angeles," made of oranges, can clearly be seen under the bell. Surrounding the Liberty Bell were displays of lemons, oranges, shaddocks, and grapefruits from Ventura and San Bernardino counties.

The Orange as Entertainment

In the 1870s, when the orange was exceptional, expensive, and exotic to most Americans, citrus growing held a fascination for immigrants to California, many of whom had owned other types of orchards in the Midwest and East. To capitalize on this curiosity and to give growers a chance to compete for prizes for both their fruit and displays, A.S. White and H.J. Rudisill organized the first California citrus-themed fair in Riverside in 1879. Among the fruit exhibited at this show were some very early examples of what would eventually become known as the Washington navel. The show attracted hundreds of people from throughout the area and became an annual event. Citrus fairs, Kevin Starr notes, were a way for the agricultural colonists of California to "create . . . a culture of themselves."

Ghosts of Oranges Past. The first California—and possibly the world's—citrus fair was held in February 1879, in Riverside, sponsored by the Southern California Horticultural Society. A special pavilion was built for the event in 1882 and the shows were there held annually until 1891, when San Bernardino staged its first citrus fair in a new, larger exhibit hall. That show became the much more ambitious National Orange Show in 1911. These undated images are from stereopticon cards labeled only "Riverside."

The National Orange Show

By far the biggest, longest-running, and most significant citrus fair began in 1911. The National Orange Show in San Bernardino was the idea of a professional ice skater and entertainer, Harry Perkins. With support from the San Bernardino Chamber of Commerce, Perkins fashioned the National Orange Show into part theme park, part tradeshow, part agricultural exposition, and part theater "as a means of encouraging the culture of citrus fruits and promoting the distribution of the exotic crop throughout the world."[34] The governor of California pushed a button in Sacramento that set off fireworks and lit flashing lights over the entrance. Three thousand people attended the first year, and a hundred boxes of fruit were on display. Ten years later, attendance had grown to 150,000, and the show featured thousands of oranges fashioned into "A Wondrous and Enchanting Spectacle of Gold." By the late 1940s, promotional materials declared that "attendance tops the 350,000 mark annually."

Billed as "California's Greatest Midwinter Event," and promoted as "national in scope—international in its interest," the National Orange Show introduced a new theme every year. In 1932, the show commemorated George Washington's two-hundredth birthday *and* the Olympic Games, which were coming to Los Angeles that year. In 1937, a "Gay Hollywood" theme featured more than seventy thousand square yards of "expensive satins, broadcloths and velours" that transformed the building into "movieland magnificence." And, in 1950, "Once Upon a Time" was adopted to "inspire artists" to bring "a delectable atmosphere of fantasy and romance."

A specially commissioned march in 1926 captured the exuberance of the National Orange Show. One newspaper reported, "Tourists, prospectors, foreign visitors, rich and poor, farmers, orchardists, merchants, retired businessmen—all mingling in one big joyous ensemble . . . It is a big, fine, bounding success, overflowing with life and ginger and interest."

Municipalities, along with other civic and commercial groups, erected elaborate displays tied to the year's theme. Each display incorporated hundreds or thousands of oranges, and the displays became increasingly more involved over the years. They often featured actors or models who used the displays as if they were stage sets and gave theatrical performances or interacted with the spectators. Held in March, and much like the highly ritualized Pasadena Rose Parade, the National Orange Show showed off California's mild winter climate and agricultural abundance to the still-snowbound rest of the country. In the land of movies, radio, and eventually television, the orange had reached the pinnacle of success: the orange was a Star.

Fantasyland—Expositions and Orange Shows

Could the woman on this program cover be Queen Calafia? The program for the second year of the National Orange Show contains ads for automobiles, citrus machinery, fertilizer, New York stage shows, banks, hotels, and lithographers' crate label design and printing.

Publicity, public relations, positioning. The terms have evolved, but the objective has remained the same: tell the best story possible by emphasizing the positive. The National Orange Show portrayed the orange in California as symbolic, inspirational, important, exotic, and entertaining. The February 19, 1912, Evening Herald *declared, "There are tons, acres, oceans of fruit. All who come are given fruit. Everywhere the eye rests on fruit—piled in boxes, laid in rows, decorating fantastic designs, covering figures and models of everything from a flag to a locomotive and cars."*

The Orange and the Dream of California

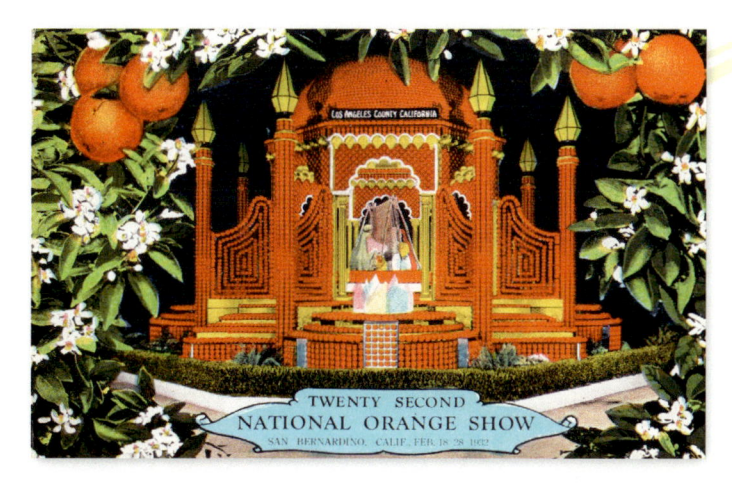

Souvenir luggage sticker from the 1928 National Orange Show.

An exposition of rare beauty— a scene from a Fairyland— nowhere else in the whole world such a dazzling sight.

Poster stamps, postage stamp-like stickers, were heavily collected in the early twentieth century. This 1917 stamp features the image used on posters and other advertising for the seventh annual National Orange Show.

LEFT BOTTOM: *In the long and practiced tradition of California dream-making, the 1929 National Orange Show mixed a fictionalized version of California's past to promote its present. The caption on this postcard reads: "Dolores Del Rio, famed Mexican star, daughter of the Dons, recognized by the citrus industry as the symbol and spirit of Southern California, and film patroness of the great show."*

Fantasyland—Expositions and Orange Shows

79

"King Orange and the entire exotic royal Citrus family bask in aureate magnificence amid a setting of myriad gorgeous fantasies at this annual exposition," reads the inside of a souvenir pictorial.

Among the attractions at the National Orange Show were stage shows, a "fun zone" of carnival rides, "top-notch screen, stage, television and radio stars," and "the world's largest fruit juice bar."

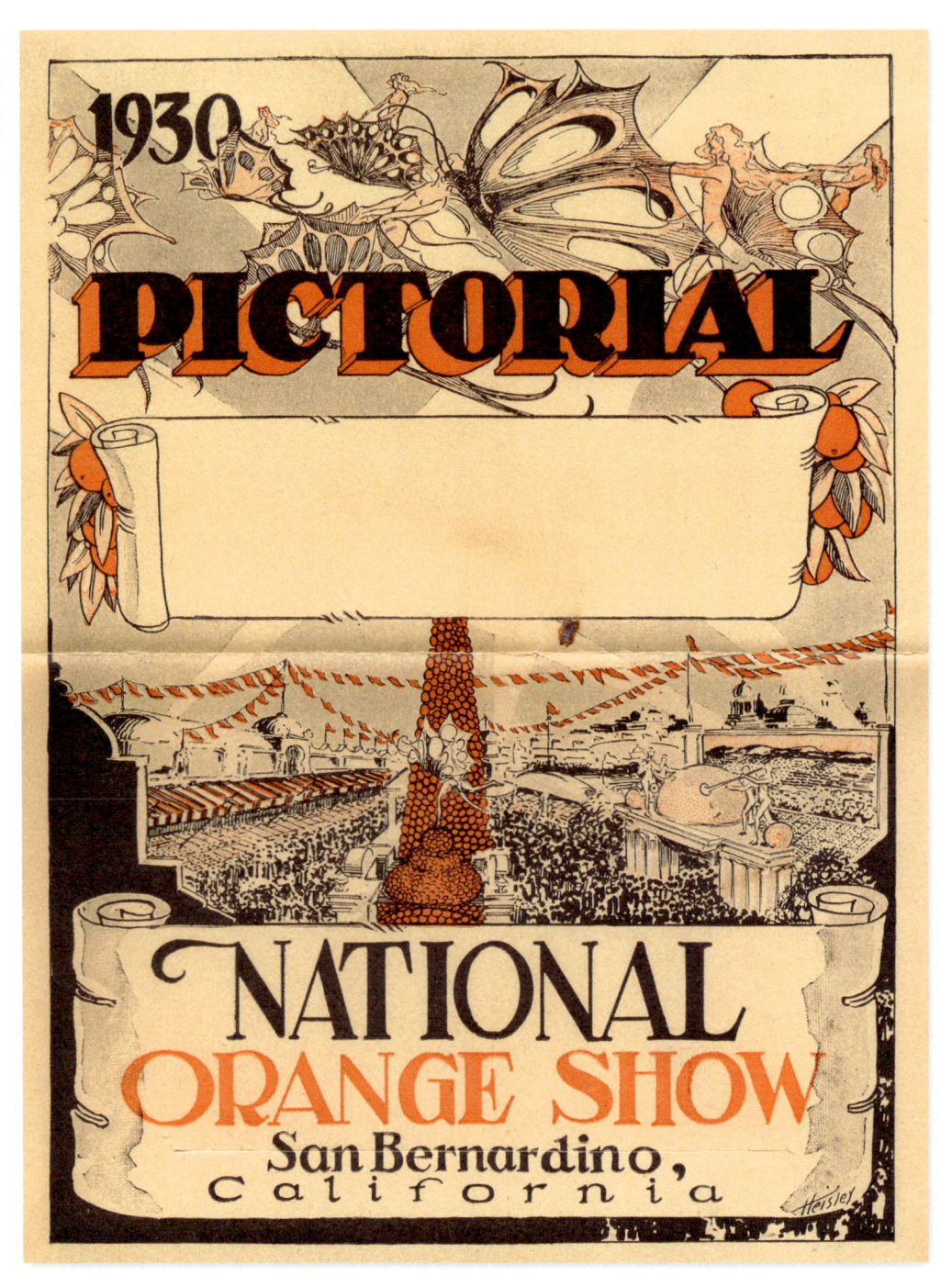

The Orange and the Dream of California

TOP: *A brochure for the 1939, twenty-ninth annual National Orange Show: "Exhibits are shown from the State, Counties, and numerous enterprising towns which are proud to be in the citrus area. These displays are especially beautiful at night under the lighting effects designed by specialists . . . The industrial exhibits are of great interest, too. New things for the office of the business man, new ideas for the homemaker, new materials for building, and new furnishings for the forward-looking young people are displays everybody enjoys . . . There will be entertainment in song and dance . . . The Midway 'concessions' make a zone of fun and frolic which especially appeals to the young, and to those who stay young."*

BOTTOM: *The National Orange Show was held in a building constructed just for the show. As the popularity of the show increased, so did the size of the building which eventually expanded to 140,000 square feet. Advertisements touted "paved automobile highways from all parts of Southern California, and through trains of the Pacific Electric Railway, lead directly to the main entrance of the National Orange Show."*

Fantasyland—Expositions and Orange Shows

81

The National Orange Show included a complete packinghouse where fruit was cleaned, graded, sorted and packed for shipment. Visitors could arrange for a whole crate of California oranges to be shipped anywhere in the country, capped with a special, limited edition National Orange Show label.

*Magnificent exhibits created by noted artists, circled by the
world's greatest citrus fruit and enhanced by a sizzling floral display:
a vast exhibit auditorium transformed
into a wondrous and enchanting spectacle of gold!*

Written in 1949 by songwriter Dave Franklin, "California Orange Blossom" was recorded by popular big-band leader Russ Morgan, pressed in rare orange vinyl, and given to radio stations to promote the National Orange Show. Franklin also wrote the theme song to the Looney Tunes cartoon series, and Morgan has a star on the Hollywood Walk of Fame.

Fantasyland—Expositions and Orange Shows

83

Second Banana—the Valencia Orange Show

The Washington navel was King Citrus in California, even though the Valencia variety was grown in almost equal numbers. Thriving away from the foothills, closer to the coast, and ripening in the spring and summer instead of the fall and winter, the Valencia was the perfect complement to the navel. The combination meant that it was orange season in California 365 days a year.

The Valencia Orange Show used a similar template as the National Orange Show: flamboyant displays constructed of millions of oranges and a something-for-everybody mélange. Held in a tent, the Valencia show was staged in late spring in Anaheim, the center of the Valencia orange empire. The event ran from 1921 to 1931.

Visitors to the Valencia Orange Show could buy crates of fresh, sweet oranges wrapped in specially printed, souvenir tissues. This tissue and logo are from the 1928 show and promote an orange packing contest.

Orange show promoters were endlessly creative in their efforts to showcase the orange as entertainment. This publicity photo for the Valencia Orange Show promotes a midsummer's night fantasy of pixies among the orange blossoms.

84

ABOVE: *This newspaper ad for the 1928 Valencia Orange Show promised "bewitching displays—mythical characters—elaborate events—a magnificent spectacle," all centered on the theme of "Enchanted Story Land." Parking for five thousand cars was available, along with special service to the show by the Motor Transit Company and Pacific Electric Railway.*

TOP RIGHT: *The Evening Express newspaper reporting on the seventh annual Valencia Orange Show: "From ridge pole to orange racks the canvas overhead is draped with soft satiny material in blue and gold, festooned with great ropes of flowers intertwined with silver and gold tinsel."*

CENTER RIGHT: *A postal cachet cover is an envelope with a design—officially printed or with one-of-a-kind artwork—commemorating a special event. This cachet cover was airmailed on opening day of the ninth annual Valencia Orange Show.*

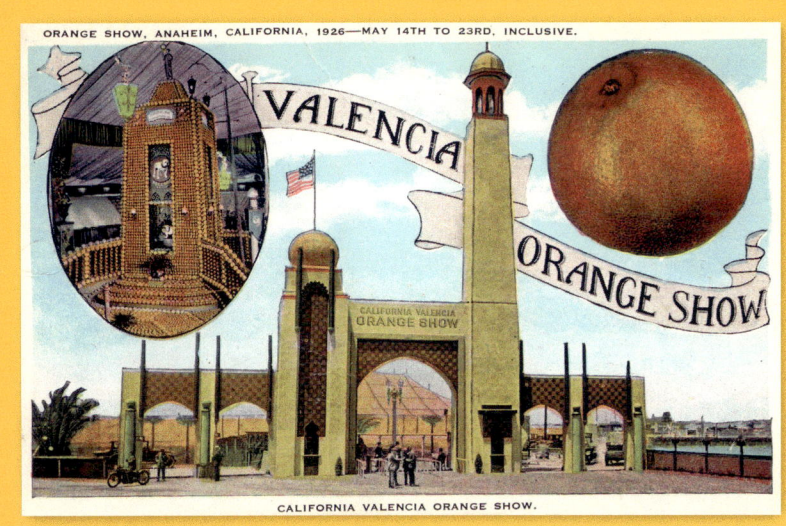

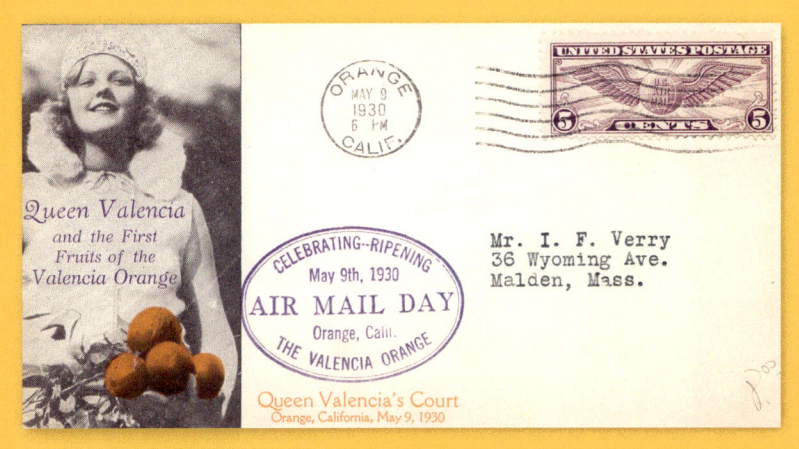

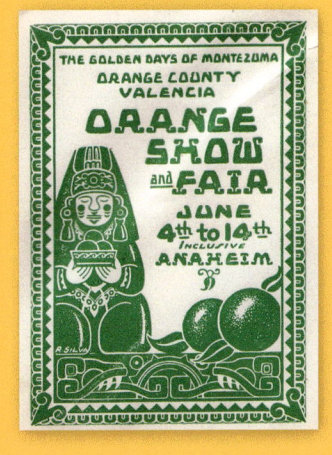

In 1931, the final year for the Valencia Orange Show, the theme was "The Golden Days of Montezuma," using the tried and true California-booster formula of mixing an exotic past to sell the present.

Fantasyland—Expositions and Orange Shows

85

*The romanticized portrayal in magazines writing on California citriculture at the time often ignored,
as Mark Wyman noted his 2010 book* Hoboes: Bindlestiffs, Fruit Tramps, and the Harvesting of the West,
"not only the difficulties and dangers facing workers, but the many tasks required to keep citrus groves producing."

6

Love's Labour's Lost— The People, Skills, Machines and Hard Work Needed to Bring Paradise to the Table

Orange culture pays but it pays at the expense of the most careful, painstaking attention and unremitting labor.
ALLAN SUTHERLAND
"Orange Culture in Southern California," *The Booklovers Magazine*, 1904

The promotion of California's orange empire was like a lovingly staged set in an ornate theater. But past the proscenium, secreted behind the scrim, were heavy machinery and toiling people who made the fantasy seem possible. The boosters and believers would say "pay no attention" to those behind the curtain, but the California dream of peace and plenty would never have seemed so real without enormous apparatus and extraordinary labor.

The soil is there, of untold productiveness, waiting to yield bounteous harvest as soon as it is vitalized by moisture.
Land of Sunshine: Southern California—
An authentic description of its natural features, resources and prospects, 1893

WATER

It began with water, or rather the lack of it. Fertile soil and remarkable climate were not enough; water was needed to make California blossom. California's low-lying inland valleys, where oranges grew most successfully, are near desert-like terrain. Water cooperatives, water districts, water companies, and water lawsuits were an integral part of the orange's development in California. With the exuberance and flamboyance typical of those who were coming under the spell of California, D.B. Weir captured the importance of water to the growing of oranges in an 1893 article for *California Illustrated Magazine*:

> When the secret of the soil's fertility—a secret which nature had so long kept guarded under the unattractive covering of parched sage and grease bush—was discovered and understood, the scene was rapidly changed, and the rich soil, riotous in the exuberance of delight at escape from the bondage of aridity, burst out into productiveness on a scale that drove men wild with excitement. They had found out that with irrigation those dry, barren lands could be converted into gardens of Hesperides.

Irrigation had brought a million formerly arid acres into bloom by 1890 and another five million by 1930. This effort required, pointed out Douglas Sackman in the 2005 book Orange Empire: California and the Fruits of Eden, *more than "500,000 pumps, 46,000 pumping plants, 4,000 dams and reservoirs, and 32,000 miles of pipelines and canals."*

Such enthusiasm overlooked the exhaustive effort involved in building the aqueducts, reservoirs, canals, pipes, sluices, and ditches needed to bring the magic elixir of water to the dark-leaved trees with golden fruit. The towns and terminals envisioned by developers and utopian-inspired entrepreneurs, such as John North's 1870 Southern California Colony Association in the California desert, which would eventually become Riverside, and the 1873 Indiana Colony further west, which would become Pasadena in 1886, first began with the securing of water and water rights.

"God never intended Southern California to be anything but desert,"
a visitor once remarked. "Man has made it what it is."
CAREY MCWILLIAMS
Southern California: An Island on the Land, 1946

"Not since ancient Rome or the creation of Holland had any society comparably subdued, appropriated, and rearranged its water resources."[35]

Love's Labour's Lost

More Water, More Oranges

The connection between water and the California orange was so strong that over several decades one image was used over and over for a popular souvenir postcard: a picture of a perfectly manicured orchard being irrigated. The startling difference, though, is that every time the card was reprinted it featured a remarkably different number of ripe oranges on the trees, from none to uncountable. Odd and interesting. The retouchers had their way with the clouds, too.

90

The Orange and the Dream of California

The newcomer who starts into the orange growing business must not . . .
think that all he has to do is plant the trees
and then sit down and reap the golden harvest.
"Orange Growing," *Land of Sunshine*, July 1894

Labor

From teachers to movie stars, shopkeepers to bankers, office workers to factory workers, a wide swath of Californians tried their hand at citriculture during its golden years. A large percentage of the groves were small, five to ten acres, and were owned and operated as a supplement to the grower's full-time occupation. The manageability of such modest-sized groves reinforced the popular image of orange growing as a way for "hard-working, community-minded individuals" to build an "alternative to either the isolation of rural life or the 'hustle and bustle' of the modern industrial city." These growers did not see themselves as dirt farmers tethered to the soil and struggling for hardscrabble returns, but referred to themselves as horticulturists and orchardists. They took pleasure in characterizing their efforts as a way, described by Starr in *California*, "to amalgamate the genteel tradition and the strenuous life."

There was, however, a conspicuous contradiction in the California citriculture idealism. While many people believed in the Progressive Era ideals of their times, they also had a distinctly provincial worldview. The lofty rhetoric of building virtuous, healthy, high-minded communities did not extend to the inclusion of other cultures, races, or classes. It wasn't particularly greed or mindful self-interest that fostered these views, but an us-and-them outlook—reflective of the era—that resulted in a sometimes patronizing and often exploitative approach to labor relations.

When the missions were secularized in 1834, Native Americans were the region's commercial workforce, and "readily shifted over to the American colony settlements."[36] They had the knowledge and skills required to keep the fledgling California agricultural promise continuing. Then, in the first great growth of orange planting, and just as their work in mining and building

The romance of the orange and the dream of California were woven together to promote the possibility of an agrarian utopia made up of prosperous family farms anchored by a cooperative, cultured community, resulting in a "genteel bohemian lifestyle." The sender of this 1909 card wrote on the back, "This is God's country."

the transcontinental railroads was coming to end, Chinese workers replaced much of the field labor force. Citrus had been cultivated for centuries in southern China, and many of the Chinese immigrants were "more familiar with Citriculture than the American Midwesterners"[37] who had also immigrated to California and who owned the orchards. Chinese workers made up eighty percent of the citrus labor force by 1885.

The first national immigration law, the Chinese Exclusion Act in 1882, and the subsequent 1888 Scott Act, which denied reentry of Chinese laborers who left the United States, resulted in a critical shortage of workers. Even a small grove was labor intensive and required—especially by absentee owners and large-scale operators—a year round, experienced, knowledgeable workforce. Agriculture work shifted to new groups. The Japanese were the largest citrus labor group in the early twentieth century, joined by Filipino, Sikh, and Anglo laborers. Eventually Mexican workers became predominant, with "women working as packers and men in the fields."[38]

David Vaught, in *Cultivating California: Growers, Specialty Crops and Labor*, observes that "our perceptions . . . have been limited to two dimensions: as avid believers in the family farm, or as people devoid of any . . . culture whatsoever except the desire to . . . maximize profits." The tension between the need for highly specialized agricultural labor and the challenges of growers has been a central part of California history. In 1936, deep in the Great Depression, when, as Gustavo Arellano described it in his 2009 magazine piece, "race and class were inseparable" and "radicalism was in the air," this tension erupted into violent conflict. Half of Orange County's Mexican naranjeros, crucial citrus-picking workers, went on strike for higher wages and the right to unionize. Law enforcement reacted viciously and the news media hysterically, labeling the strikers as "a bunch of communists." Carey McWilliams, in *Southern California: an Island on the Land*, reported his "astonishment in discovering how quickly social power could crystallize into an expression of

Sent in 1921 by an orange grove owner to a friend in Wisconsin, this postcard teases, "Wouldn't you like to help pick our oranges?" A five-acre California orange grove was capable of producing the profit equal to a two-hundred-acre Midwest farm, noted Hal Barron in the Spring, 1995 issue of California History.

arrogant brutality in these lovely, seemingly placid . . . communities."

The truth is, as Vaught put it, "horticulture was no more virtuous an undertaking than . . . any other type of farming. . . . Day after day, year after year, growers confronted problems that would have baffled most contemporary industrialists, including small-scale—but intensive—production, seasonal and environmental pressures, intricate labor systems, distant markets, community relations." Pierre Laszlo concludes, in *Citrus: A History*, "both exploited labor and visionary great men contributed to the citrus boom." Reality is complex; myths are specific, clear, comfortable.

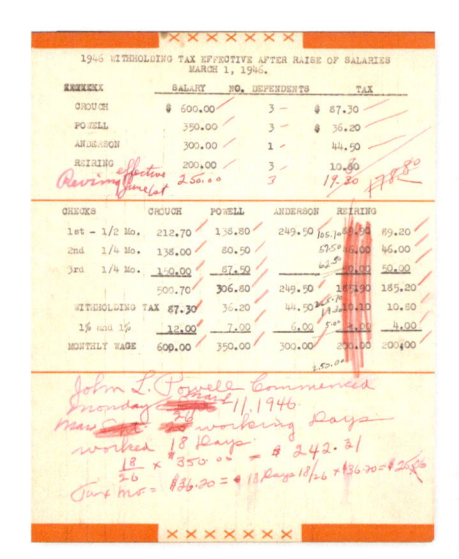

LEFT: *This timecard from a Whittier California packinghouse calibrates employee wages and taxes-owed after a "raise in salaries."*

BOTTOM: *Orange growing is intensive farming; an orange orchard of any size requires hard work, and lots of it. The effort is continuous: planting, pruning, disease prevention, frost protection, watering, picking, packing, and, finally, shipping.*

Chinese and then Japanese immigrants made up much of the labor in the early days of California citriculture development. Many of these workers had citrus and other agricultural experience before coming to the United States, and their knowledge and skills played a critical role in the rapidly growing industry. Both Chinese and Japanese pickers, packers, and fieldworkers organized under contractors and had some success in securing wage increases.

Love's Labour's Lost

Planting

All California orange trees were, in the beginning, grown from seed. Seedling trees can take fifteen years to mature and bear at full capacity. This meant a long wait before the investment made by orchard owners could begin to be recovered. In the 1870s, nurserymen started to experiment with budded varieties from Australia, China, England, Japan and South America. Budding means the trees are made of two parts: a robust root stock variety to which another kind—that will produce the desired type of fruit—is grafted. A budded tree starts producing well in just five years. Over a hundred budded types were tried, but only a handful adapted well to California and were found to be superior to seedling varieties. The Mediterranean Sweet from Europe was the first to prove of value and was extensively planted.

In an article, "The Orange in Northern California," (*Scientific American,* February 21, 1903), Enos Brown states: "From the time of planting the first seedlings, the land is cultivated without much cessation. February, March, and April are the months when the ground is plowed and cross-plowed . . . Under the trees is cultivated by gangs of men. February and March is the time for pruning. All low and superfluous growth is then cut down . . . Ditches are run between the rows and three feet distant from the trees, three ditches between each row. Water is supplied at least once each month and for twenty-four hours at a time. After each irrigation, a harrow is run over the ground and the temporary ditches leveled. May, June, July, August, September, and October are devoted to cultivation and general oversight. In November, the fruit begins to mature, and all else is dropped in order to gather the crop. The gathering season is in full operation by the middle of the month, when the labor of every man, woman, and child is utilized for picking, packing, and shipping the ripe fruit. This essential matter being concluded, the season is over and the orchardist is permitted a rest."

There are many perplexing problems which the orange grower has to face: whether to plant early or late, to prune high or low, what fertilizer to use, what method of irrigation to follow, and how to guard against frost and heat, insects, and natural diseases of the trees.

Allan Sutherland
"Orange Culture in Southern California," *The Booklovers Magazine,* 1904

The Orange and the Dream of California

I Can See (un)Clearly Now—
Smudge Pots and How They Saved the Orange

The temperature can fall to below freezing in California's celebrated Mediterranean-like climate. As John McCarthy described in a 1940 journal article: "A heavy frost could ruin a whole crop of fruit. A severe frost could ruin an orchard." After the brutal freezes of 1883 and, especially, 1913, which recorded two of the coldest nights ever (a chilling 17 and 7 degrees, respectively) in greater Los Angeles, growers began experimenting with ways to protect their groves.

Along with a lot of oranges, California was producing a lot of oil. Oil was cheap, and oil-burning orchard heaters were developed. Called smudge pots, the earliest examples produced not only warmth, but thick, black smoke. For sixty years this smoke was pervasive across orange-growing areas. Eventually return-stack heaters were developed that produced less smoke, but more heat and wind currents. Research showed that it was the heat—not smoke—that was working and that frost could also be prevented by circulating the air at five to seven miles an hour. Most types of smudge pots were outlawed in 1947.

"This is the Fruit Frost Service. The temperatures in the following areas will be below freezing: Anaheim 26, Covina 23, La Habra 24, Pomona 24, Walnut 24 . . ."

During the winter, radios across the citrus belt were turned every night at eight o'clock to station KFI, where the national network feed was interrupted by the flat, unemotional reading of area temperatures by Floyd D. Young, U.S. Weather Bureau meteorologist and the voice of the Southern California Fruit Frost Warning Service. What he reported determined whether families and citrus workers went to bed or would work all night to save their crops.

LEFT: *An average of fifty smudge pots were used per acre, although groves at the chilly base of the San Gabriel Mountains might take twice that many.*

RIGHT: *A 1937 newsletter paints a vivid picture of the war citrus growers waged against frost: "Elderly men are there, keeping an experienced eye on the situation. Young men are there, strong and efficient in their work to be done. Youth is there, in the hundreds of high school boys called to the fray. Women are there, working side by side with fathers, husbands, and brothers. Or carrying on alone, shouldering the responsibility with only the assistance of younger children. In the homes they are busy preparing hot lunches, coffee, and sandwiches for the toiling ones. Childhood is there, with tots of tender age begging to stay up, going out happily with Mother to carry a hot lunch to Daddy at midnight."*

Love's Labour's Lost

Picking

Citrus-grove work was strenuous and constant. Ripe fruit was available to be picked in California virtually all year: Washington navels in the winter, Valencias in the summer, and lemons and other varieties in between. In his 1882 *Orange Culture in California*, Thomas Garey noted, "An inexperienced or careless hand will generally do more damage to the trees in one day's work than a skilled workman would do in a whole year." Growers learned this quickly and implemented standard practices for the hand-picking of their fruit, including having workers wear gloves, never pulling the oranges off the tree, using special blunt-nosed clippers that prevented piercing the orange's skin, and clipping the stem close to the fruit so it couldn't mar other oranges. Growers also began paying workers by the day, not by the box, to encourage careful handling. When full, pickers emptied their heavy canvas shoulder bags into field boxes, which were kept in cool storage while awaiting the oranges next step: washing, sorting, packing.

Period descriptions of the skills needed, and number of workers required, to maintain an orchard vary to a remarkable and disconcerting degree. A 1903 *Scientific American* article says "the methods pursued by orange cultivators . . . are such as anyone, even though not experienced in the business, can easily acquire," and that "ordinarily one man to thirty-five acres" is all that is needed. But a different view is offered in a 1904 article, *Orange Culture in Southern California*, which reported "this work gives employment to many thousands." And a 1924 issue of *Nature Magazine* states "harvesting the orange crop is a distinct industry . . . often done by organized crews instead of the grower himself." The paradoxical perspectives of myth and reality often collided.

"One man can care for twenty acres of bearing orange orchard. The necessary experience is easily acquired," reported Harry Ellington Brook in his 1893 pamphlet, The Land of Sunshine: Southern California—An authentic description of its natural features, resources and prospects." *Other period accounts gave a less breezy review of the effort required to successfully manage an orange orchard, warning of choosing poor land, the wrong variety, water challenges, insect pests and the critical need for experienced labor.*

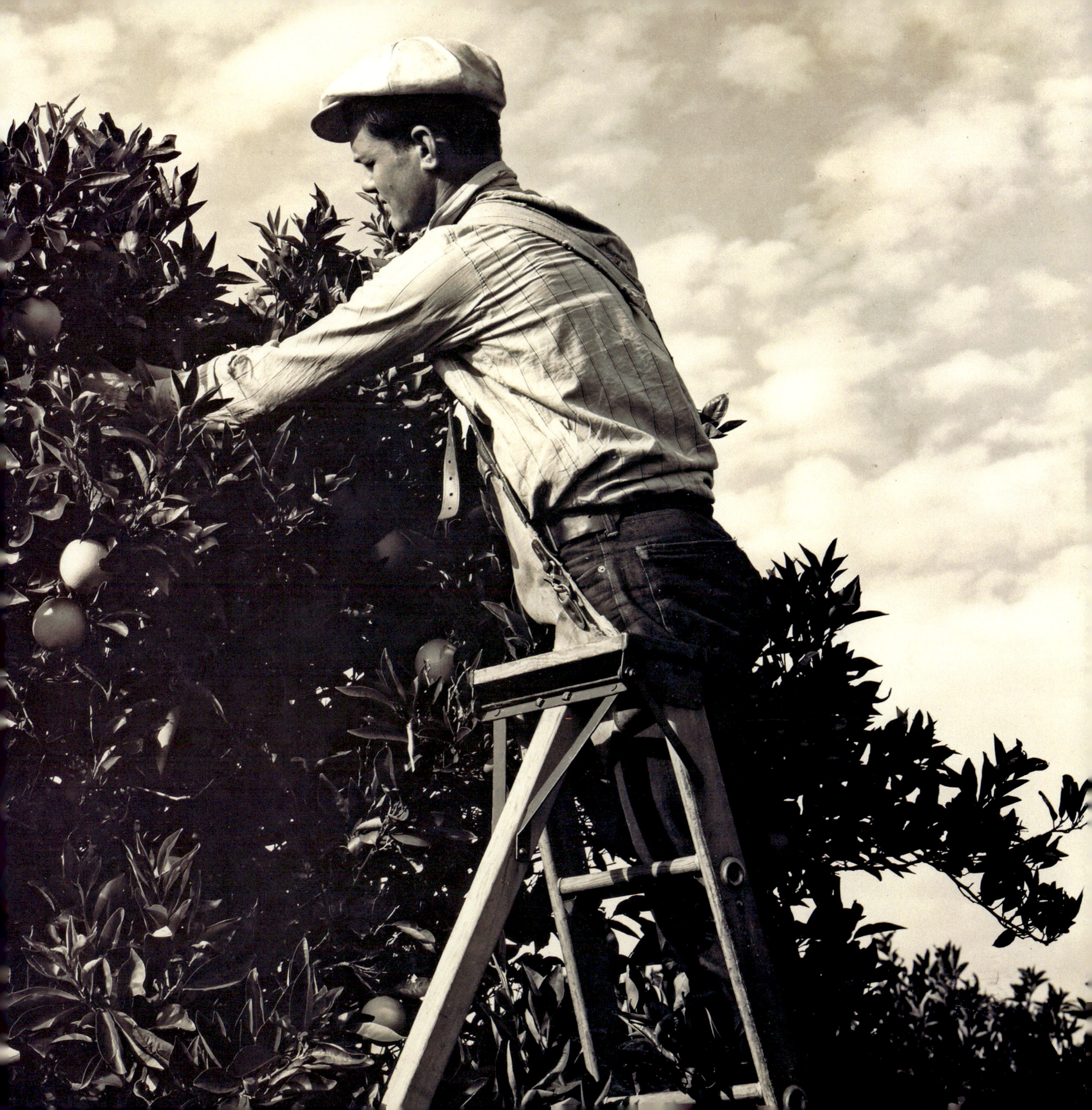

9981. The Orange Pickers, Los Angeles, California.

100

The Orange and the Dream of California

An Orange Love Story

Grace May Rowland and William C. Hahn met while working at a California packinghouse in the early 1900s. Their story reflects those of many people who came to California to find health, employment, and a better life among the oranges.

Grace was born in Indian Territory (Oklahoma, before it was a state) in 1895. Her dad died from an infected tooth, and her mother sold the family store, packed up her four children and moved to Fullerton, California, to be near her sister. Another reason for moving west: Grace's mother didn't want her only son to have to go to work in the local lead mines.

William came with his mother and two half-sisters from Michigan, when his mother was diagnosed with a "lung problem," and the doctor prescribed the California climate as a cure.

Grace worked packing oranges at the C.C. Chapman packinghouse in Orange County after graduating from high school, where she'd taken "a four-year course in business." She earned two dollars a day. She wrote in her memoir, "I had very few boyfriends; no one had any money to take or go places."

William worked for Mr. Chapman as chauffer. One of his jobs was to drive a seven-passenger touring car and pick-up and deliver the young women who worked at the packinghouse. Grace says she "always sat in the front seat by the driver."

Grace and William married in 1916. William became an electrician for Fox Film Corporation and worked there for forty years—long after the merger with Twentieth Century Pictures that formed Twentieth Century-Fox. Grace worked as a school secretary until their children were born. She never learned to drive a car, but for the rest of her life with William, she always made sure to sit in the front seat, by the driver.

For Grace and William, the dream had become reality.

Grace received this pin when she attended a convention while in high school.

Love's Labour's Lost

101

At the packinghouse, the oranges are cordially welcomed with a warm bath and the swish of soft brushes, followed by a cold shower, then away to be dried by air blast and graded.

CHARLES WILSON
"Oranges—Our Golden Wealth," *Nature Magazine*, 1924

PACKING

California citrus labor reflected the social, political, and racial attitudes of the era; work was often segregated by gender, class, ethnicity. As Margo McBane described in the Spring, 1995 *California History*, "Religion and class divided jobs between skilled and unskilled workers." Women most often had the job of sorting and carefully packing the fruit.

There were hundreds of purpose-built packinghouses across southern California and along the Sierra foothills. Citrus growing was a collectively organized enterprise, and the packinghouses provided large and small growers alike the specialized facilities, machinery, and labor required for preparing their crops for shipping to market. Only a portion of the oranges delivered to the packinghouses were able to meet the requirements for being classified and packed as premium grade fruit, so packers were tasked with sorting millions of oranges into the appropriate bins and crates.

Working in the packinghouses, points out Gilbert Gonzalez in his 1995 piece, "Women, Work, and Community in Mexican *Colonias*" in the journal *California History*, women "often earned wages equal to those of men, thereby allowing a measure of economic and social independence. . . . Packers also enjoyed a distinc-

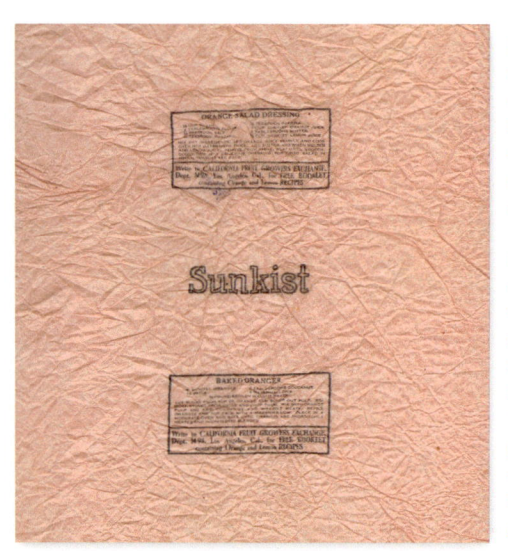

LEFT: *Packinghouse workers individually wrapped each orange in tissue and packed the crates according to a precise arrangement, ensuring a consistent number of oranges in each.*

RIGHT: *Tissues like this helped ensured safe transport of California oranges across thousands of miles and weeks of transport. This one identified the orange inside as premium "Sunkist" quality, had recipes printed on it, and could be collected with others and redeemed for premiums like a juice extractor or silverware.*

tive social life within the packinghouse. Birthdays . . . and other special events were often celebrated . . . with potlucks and parties." This world, with its routines, culture, and challenges, ended after World War II, as California's population soared, and the orange groves and packinghouses disappeared to make way for houses, shopping centers, and theme parks.

These women are packing lemons, but the work of carefully sorting and crating any type of citrus was much the same and performed in similar surroundings.

Love's Labour's Lost

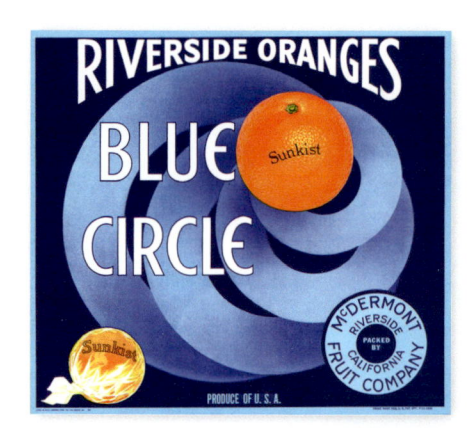

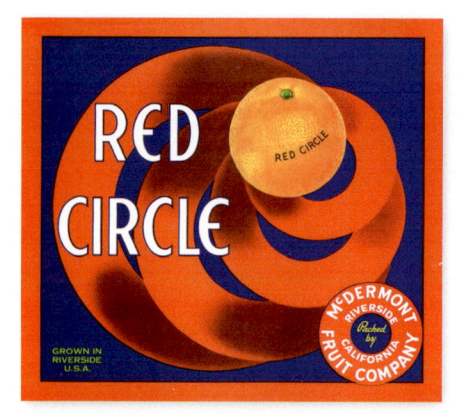

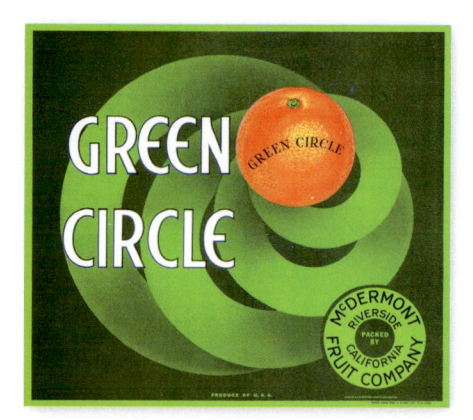

Oranges grown in the same orchard typically varied in quality and size. Most producers divided and packed their oranges into at least three grades, often using colors or related brand names on the box labels to designate the different quality levels. The McDermont Fruit Company in Riverside had the Blue Circle brand with Sunkist identification, as its premium brand, Red Circle as its intermediate grade, and Green Circle for its lowest quality.

This image from a large-format glass slide was part of a series on California used in schools and for public lectures. Even the tedious work of sorting and packing oranges in warehouses was photographed as glamorously as if the worker were a movie star.

*These orange and lemon workers are, in one sense,
the direct descendants of the New England mill girls of forty years earlier.
One sees in their surroundings the same toil of piecework, but softened somewhat
by the absence of heavy machinery and the much lighter nature of their task.*
KEVIN STARR
Inventing the Dream: California through the Progressive Era, 1985

This photograph is dated June 16, 1939, and on the back is written, "Mama aqui le mando este retrato de el empaque en donde trabajamos" *(Mama, I'm sending you this picture of where we work packing). Gilbert Gonzalez, in* California History, *quotes Angelina Cruz:* "You were so absorbed in packing that you lost track of time . . . you just kind of lost yourself."[39]

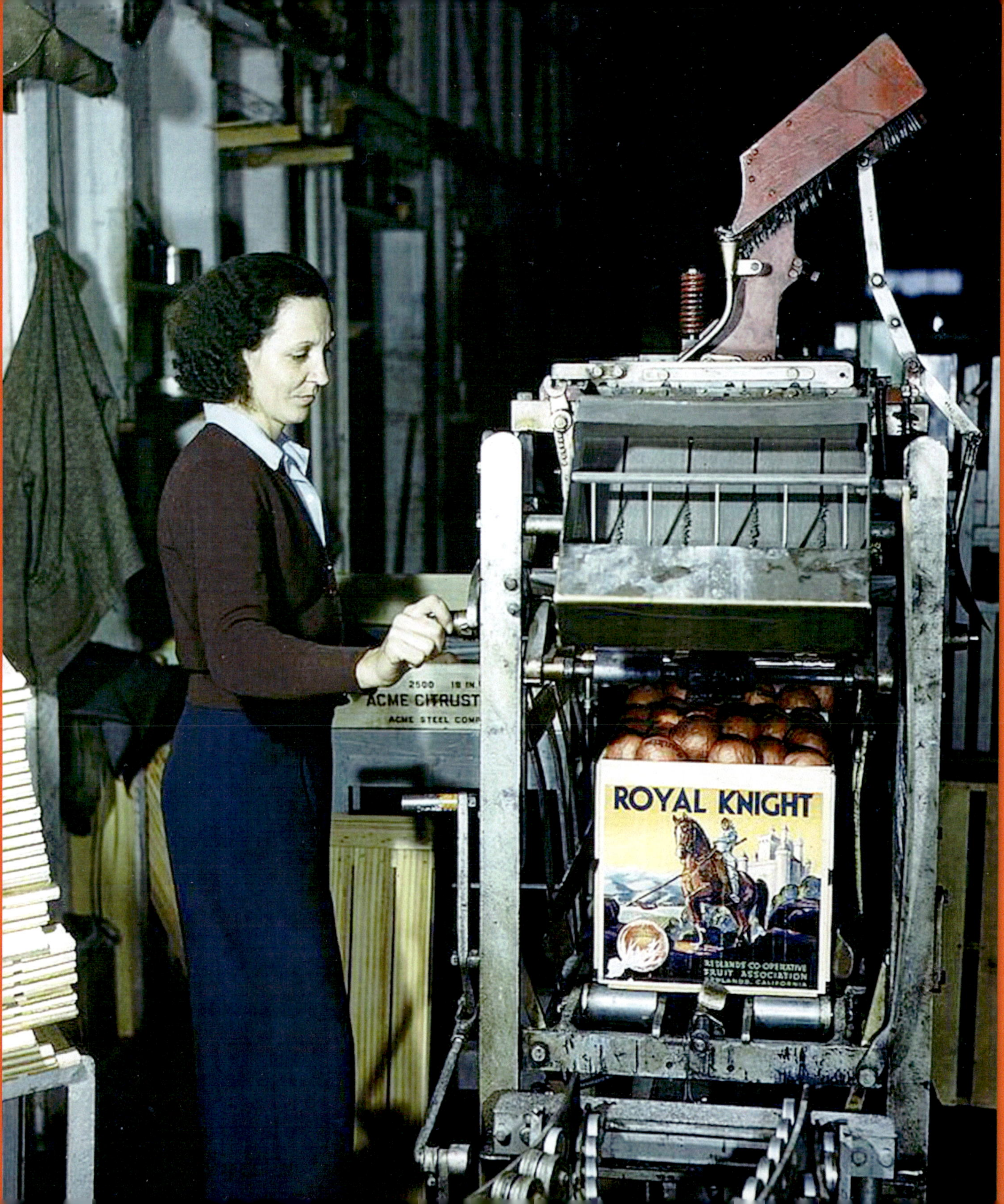
ROYAL KNIGHT

Unless we better understand the mechanical portion of life, we cannot have the time to enjoy the trees and the birds, and the flowers, and the green fields.
HENRY FORD

MACHINERY

There was an enormous amount of specialized machinery involved in citriculture, and virtually all of it came from just two men. Fred Stebler opened the California Iron Works in Riverside, California, in 1903, designing and building the washing, drying, sorting, and packing equipment. His inventions would become the standard packinghouse equipment used around the world. George Parker bought the Riverside Foundry and Machine Works in 1909 and built nailing and box-making machines as well as citrus-washing equipment. The two men were bitter rivals, and each filed numerous patent-infringement lawsuits against the other. Neither was able to triumph, and eventually they joined forces to form the Stebler-Parker Company. But it remained an uneasy relationship.

A third competitor arrived in the 1920s. Hal Paxton developed a lighter, faster nailing machine and an improved "lidding" machine. The three competing businesses were consolidated in 1938 by the Food Machinery Corporation. By then, Riverside had become the world center for citrus machinery.

Packinghouse compressor room of the La Verne Orange and Lemon Company in Lordsburg, California.

Love's Labour's Lost

LEFT: *While showing heavy machinery and manual labor, this stereopticon card was sold as part of "The California Missions and the State of California" collection. Anything to do with California's romanticized citriculture was of interest to the rest of the country.*

BOTTOM: *Spraying for citrus white fly in 1933, this State of California crew was working in Pasadena. The effort took two spray men, two hose pullers, and three hundred feet of hose.*

The founding of an orange orchard is not all poetry and romance;
the stern, cold facts and responsibilities of the industry soon become apparent.

How grand, how beautiful is an orange orchard in full bearing!
When planted artistically, their ever-enduring dark-green foliage,
studded with beautiful gems of golden spheres, give renewed life and health
to all that behold the orchards or partake of the fruit.

THOMAS GAREY
Orange Culture in California, 1882

CRAZY LIKE AN ORANGE—BIG IDEAS THAT DIDN'T WORK

These two quite different viewpoints, from the same observer in the same article, perfectly display the synthesis of myth and reality surrounding the orange in California. Even when addressing the real effort required, commentators couldn't resist poetically embellishing the work and the results.

Because so many California citriculturalists originally came from other disciplines, particularly as entrepreneurs, they were open to experimentation. Often this resulted in improved processes, efficiency, and yields, but not always.

Love's Labour's Lost

Roofer Madness

Here's an idea from the January 6, 1900 issue of *Harper's Weekly*: build a latticework roof over *all* the orange orchards in California.

What, in the opinion of leading orange-growers, is destined to revolutionize the methods of growing . . . fruit has been introduced and has successfully passed the stage of experimentation . . . Undoubtedly . . . the method will within a few years be largely adopted, and there are experts who declare that . . . every orchard in the State will have to get under roof, or the men running them will have to quit business.

It will cost many millions of dollars to cover the orange groves of California, but when this is done, the crops will be absolutely secure against failure.

A MORE SCIENTIFIC FORM OF IRRIGATION.
The orange grower now can say: "Turn on the rain."

Even more than for irrigation, this idea was conceived as a way to prevent frost damage by spraying the trees with well water that would be warmer than the air temperature. The inventor optimistically predicted that, "It would be possible for an ingenious orchardist to equip his system with a small motor, and clockwork attachment, by which the sprinklers could be turned on automatically."

RAIN-MAKING FOR THE ORANGE GROWER

Rain Man

Technical World Magazine recommended in 1912 that growers build sprinkler systems above their orchards to mimic rainfall.

Much more poetical, and infinitely more beautiful than the old-fashioned, prosaic "ditch" irrigation, is a revolutionary system of applying water to orange groves which is now being worked out in the Porterville orange district in California, in which the orchardist actually "makes it rain" at will." Citrus growers were soon convinced that "there is some subtle effect upon the vigor of the tree when it is thoroughly wet, probably upon the same general principle as the invigorating feeling when a tired man takes a bath."

Love's Labour's Lost

Risky Business

In its constant attempt to balance the scale between supply and demand, Sunkist bought a marmalade factory in 1915 and began marketing Sunkist orange and grapefruit flavors, along with Sunkist Orange Jelly. Five years later, this experiment in using excess capacity ended, and the factory was converted into an industrial-citrus-products facility when Sunkist discovered that making marmalade required very few oranges, and that most of the product and expense was in glass, sugar, and labels.

Sunkist described its product as "the New American Marmalade," made in California "where the best oranges grow."

In an era when home canning was still prevalent, Sunkist promoted its marmalade as "Cooked by Women" on "Small Stoves" for real "home taste." This method was chosen because "no man, no matter how able, was ever a cook by instinct." The appealing illustrations and copy from a period pamphlet contrast with photographs of the actual factory and the real work required.

Cooked on Small Stoves

IN FACT, we cook just the same as you cook at home when you make your own preserves.

We use small, individual gas stoves, and cook only a few pounds at a time — less than four gallons, to be exact.

Each kettle is watched individually, constantly being stirred and tested carefully, until it is done just right.

There isn't any hurry. There are no "short-cut" methods. We might cook in bulk, in 7000-lb. vats, and cut our costs immensely.

But we aim to make something different from just a "brand" of marmalade. We are making *good* marmalade with the real "home taste." So we use the costlier small stove and cook the slower way. The home cooking unit is simply duplicated scores of times in the Sunkist kitchens.

Cooked by Women

FURTHERMORE, all our cooks are women. A Scotch woman, a connoisseur of marmalades and preserves, who brought our recipes to this country, superintends the cooking.

She instituted "the small stove method," saying that it was the "only way to make *good* marmalade or jelly in *any* quantity."

She selected women-cooks exclusively as her assistants; because, "no man, no matter how able, was ever a cook by *instinct*."

Thus we have three policies — "Home Materials," "Home Stoves," and "Home Cooks"— looking to real "Home Taste."

You know what that taste is. Taste Sunkist Marmalade and you will find it there.

Love's Labour's Lost

113

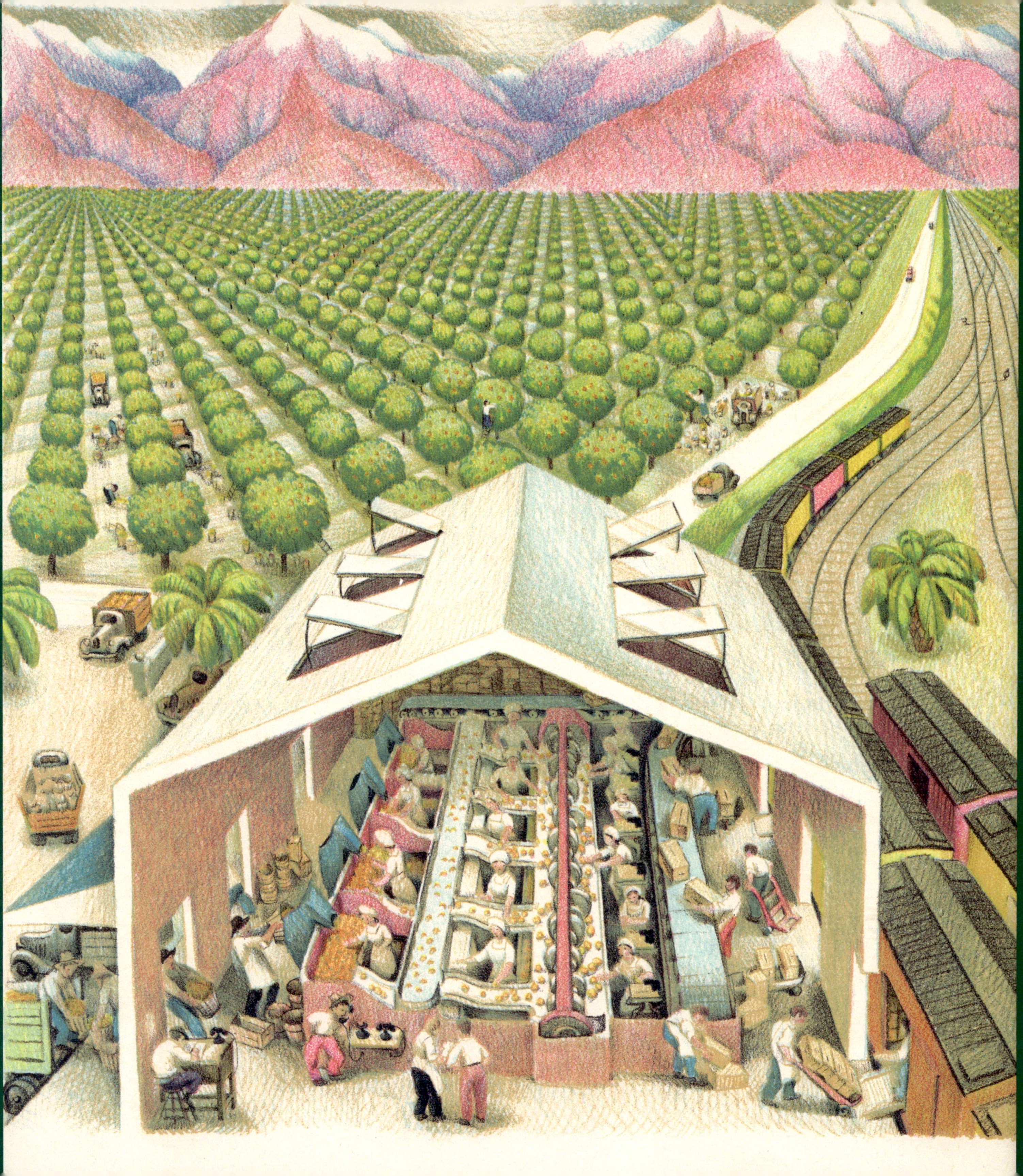

Of course, the dream outran the reality, it always does.
Kevin Starr
Americans and the California Dream, 1850-1915, 1973

Mise-en-scène

The stage stayed set. Despite the great investments of time and money; the losses and failures caused by weather, ignorance, or bad luck; the big ideas that failed; the vast infrastructure required—and, most importantly, the enormous amount of skilled, consistent, essential labor that was not often appreciated, treated decently, or even recognized—the poets and pundits of California refused to be swayed and continued to portray California and the life lived there among the oranges, as full of beauty, abundance, health, and well-being.

Perfect weather, a lovely home, beautiful trees, delicious, healthy oranges—and time to enjoy them all. The California dream.
Opposite: *From the 1944 children's book* The Story of California, *this C.H. DeWitt illustration shows California citriculture as made of lollipop-shaped trees, vivid purple mountains, and people working in harmony.*

Love's Labour's Lost

An elegant depiction of the California ideal.

7

Picture Perfect—
Orange Crate Labels

*When we come to the design of a label,
it is very easy for us to underestimate its ultimate importance.*
DON FRANCISCO, Advertising Manager, California Fruit Growers Exchange
Labels, 1918

Selling California sold oranges. Crate labels—those fragile pieces of thin paper created only to capture a wholesaler's attention and then be discarded—have survived to embody a dream. Like the literature, reporting, and ballyhoo of the same period, the labels are a wonderful combination of the fanciful and calculating, charming and commercial, direct and opaque. But most of all they are beautiful. Citrus labels are the lovely afterglow of the California orange empire.

The completion of the transcontinental railroads brought the ability to ship California products to the populated east. But this opportunity created an unprecedented challenge: how to, as Gordon McCelland described in the definitive 1985 *California Orange Box Labels,* "pack, ship, identify, and advertise a perishable product for customers who lived thousands of miles away."

Before paper labels were developed, growers, and packers identified their crop by stenciling or branding images on crate ends.

Experimentation eventually showed that a standardized, rectangular, divided wooden box was the best shipping container. When Joseph Wolfskill sent the first railroad car full of oranges to St. Louis in 1877, the boxes were branded on the ends "Wolfskill California Oranges."

But how to distinguish a difference and create a preference when the fruit was all essentially the same and, especially, when the millions of golden oranges were hidden in rough wooden boxes? The answer was to create exquisite and vivid paper labels.

Early citrus labels reflected the personal interests and pride of the pioneer California growers. Allusions to California's re-imagined Spanish and Mexican past were popular, as were images of flowers, birds, and goddesses of every description. But among the most frequently appearing were images that reflected the growing and harvesting of oranges, especially idealized portrayals featuring manicured orchards, beautiful homes, and snow-capped mountains, all warmed by spectacularly sunny skies.

Top: *Some Riverside-area growers initially used round paper labels, pasted in the center of partially stenciled box ends. Soon though, square labels, ten by twelve inches, became universal. Once these were adopted, label size did not change for seventy years.*
Bottom: *Labels like these encouraged tourism and immigration to California.*

Citrus labels reinforced the image of California heavily promoted in the popular culture of the day. Here from the prelude to the 1905 novel
The Vision of Elijah Berl, "League on league of happy homes are all but hidden by dark-leaved trees, with fruit yellow as the golden appples of the Hesperides."

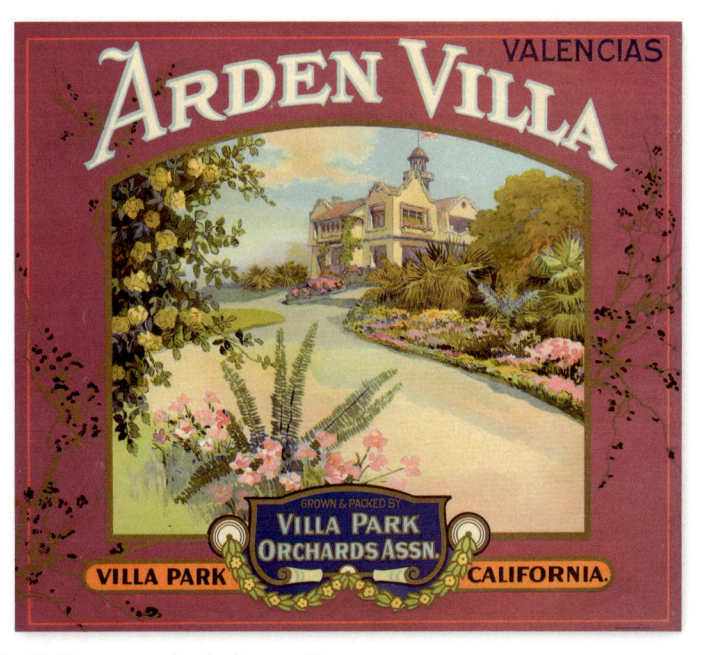

Many early labels depicted California with a Mediterranean-inspired pastoralism,
a device often adopted during this period by those selling the concept of California as paradise.

Picture Perfect—Orange Crate Labels

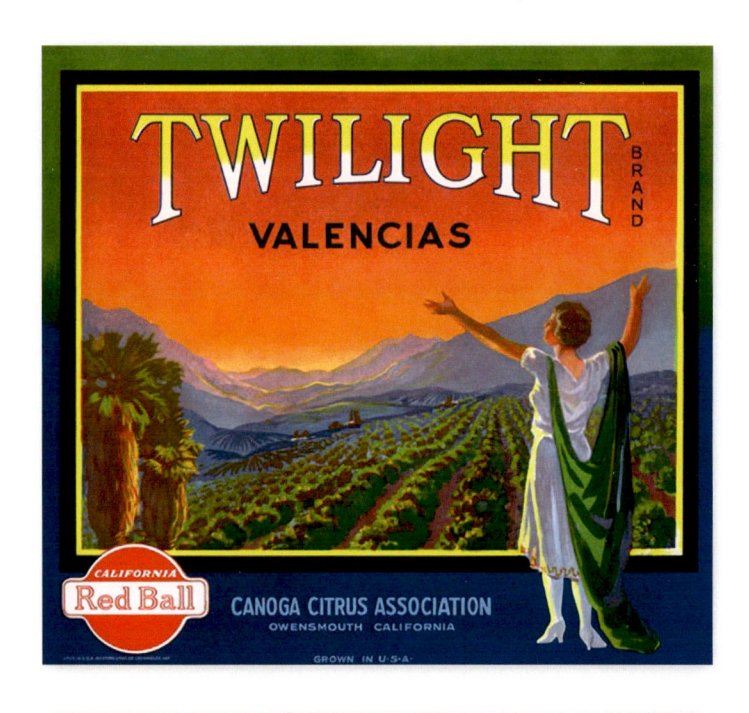

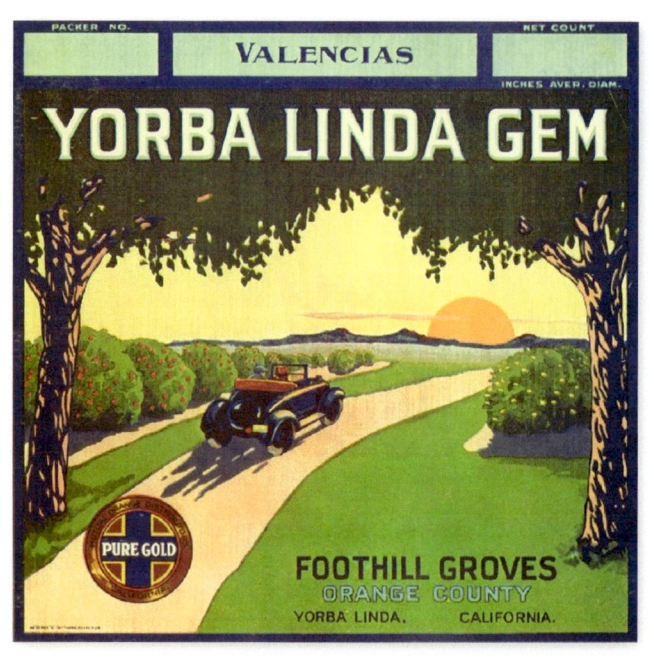

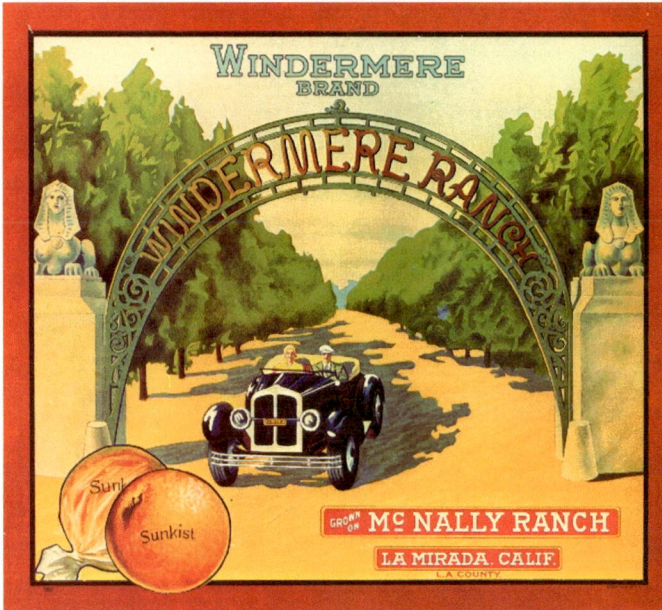

Millions across the country saw these dreamy representations as they shopped in the small grocery stores of the day, perhaps coming from a crowded city tenement or a lonely, rural farm. Together with the glowing, golden oranges displayed in these stores—often arranged in perfect pyramids—citrus labels reinforced, Kevin Starr noted, a growing, "collective image of California."

The Orange and the Dream of California

Many label lithographers produced stock labels, blanks growers could have over-printed with the name of their orchard or packinghouse.

This ad appeared on the back of the 1912 souvenir program for the second annual National Orange Show. Label printers employed highly skilled craftsmen, many trained in Europe, resulting in the remarkable technical and artistic quality of California citrus crate labels.

Commercial printers produced the citrus labels. In the early twentieth century there were more than thirty companies actively involved in California and around the country. The companies printed many millions of copies of the almost ten thousand unique label designs. While citrus labels were usually only a small part of these firms' business, the growers and packers got the benefit of the very talented artists and craftsmen working on larger jobs. Both staff and commissioned artists were used to create the illustrations and typography, but almost never signed their work; the printing companies didn't want customers to be able to pick favorites, or for the artists to demand premium compensation.

This 1912 ad is for one of the largest printers of orange crate labels. Using stone and metal plate lithography, a process called zincography, orange crate labels, notes Kevin Starr, "glowed with colors . . . that went beyond nature and spoke directly to fantasy."

Paper or Pine? During World War II, with scarcity and rationing, orange growers once again began stenciling crate box ends rather than using paper labels.

Picture Perfect—Orange Crate Labels

123

> *There is nothing distinctive about a picture of a grove . . .
> and (it) should be cautiously avoided by the shipper
> who desires to have his labels make a clear cut impression.*
>
> Don Francisco, Advertising Manager, California Fruit Growers Exchange
> *Labels,* 1918

As small-volume citriculture became more industrialized agriculture, the labels become less personal statements and more miniature billboards. Research by the California Fruit Growers Exchange in 1918 confirmed that labels should be aimed not at consumers, but at the wholesale buyer. Labels became more poster-like, with strong graphics that could be read from a distance, which emphasized the benefits of oranges and orange juice, and which featured—rather than daydreams—images of actual oranges.

By the 1950s the whole industry was evolving. Small corner grocery stores were replaced by chain supermarkets, and packinghouses were converting to cardboard cartons rather than divided wood crates. Cardboard boxes were less expensive, better suited to the increased use of fruit-packing automation and, because they were lighter, more appropriate to the new self-service shopping. The marketing value of labels had became negligible, notes Tom Spellman in the August, 2011 *Citrograph* article "The Citrus Label Era." The last California orange crate labels were printed in 1955. An art form came to an end.

124

The Orange and the Dream of California

*Spectacularly colorful, expressive, and perfectly executed, some of the most fully realized and artistically accomplished labels are the most affordable to own, simply because—
like this label from 1928—they survived in large quantities.*

ORANGE JUICE IN HAND, LET'S TOAST TO BENIGN NEGLECT

As beautiful as citrus labels are, they were produced for a utilitarian purpose: to be used and discarded. That so many survive, and many in large quantities and pristine condition, is remarkable. That they endured in such quantities was pure serendipity. The industry had contracted rapidly. Packinghouses were abandoned but left standing for years. Whatever was inside sat in dry, dark solitude, the perfect conditions for preserving paper and ink. Then, after years of disregard, an intrepid group of young graphic artists and nostalgic former growers began actively searching for and rescuing these forgotten treasures. Today, California citrus labels are appreciated by serious collectors and the casually curious, both attracted by the exceptional artistry, whimsy, color, and dreamy perfection.

Picture Perfect—Orange Crate Labels

During the golden age of Hollywood, the golden fruit was fully integrated. This 1937 publicity photo and caption promotes eating California oranges, a new Twentieth Century-Fox movie, starring child star Jane Withers, and President Roosevelt proclaiming "Child Health Day."

Ready for its Close-up—
The Orange in Hollywood

The Silver Screen and the golden fruit had much in common: both were glamorous, popular, and the things dreams are made of. Many Hollywood personalities owned orange groves as an investment and to enjoy being genteel horticulturalists—the same way many other Southern Californians did. Douglas Fairbanks had three hundred acres at Del Mar, Al Jolson ten acres in the San Fernando Valley, and Western author Zane Grey a hundred acres in the Coachella Valley, where he was member of the California Fruit Growers Exchange. Frank Capra, the six-time Academy Award winner whose films often portrayed a lyrical and idealized America, lived as a child on a California orange orchard, where his father worked as a picker.

The orange had a role in a number of Hollywood films. Stan Laurel, before he teamed with Oliver Hardy, starred in a 1923 short, *Oranges and Lemons*. He plays a California orange-grove employee named "Sunkist." Laurel, born in England, may have conceived of the film's title from the English nursery rhyme of the same name.

In the 1934 W.C. Fields movie *It's a Gift*, Fields's character lives in a

Fact and Fiction—The California Fruit Growers Exchange/Sunkist produced this consumer brochure for years, which covered the history of the orange in California, the creation of Sunkist, and the health benefits of eating and drinking citrus. W.C. Fields featured the brochure in the movie It's a Gift, *which he wrote under the pseudonym Charles Bogle.*

cramped, chaotic East Coast apartment and is beset with personal and financial problems. He dreams of moving to California and buying an orange grove where his life would be like the Sunkist brochure he carries with him everywhere. To his dismay, when he does buy an orange grove—sight unseen—and moves west with his family, he finds that not all the groves are as green and lovely as he had imagined. But, as in all California dreams, Fields does find contentment and perfection among the oranges by the time the movie ends.

And in the 1936 Charlie Chaplin masterpiece *Modern Times*, the little tramp, after being knocked unconscious, dreams that he lives in a California bungalow where he can reach out his window and pick an orange.

Film stars Mae Busch (l.) and Claire Windsor helped promote the 1923 Valencia Orange Show, held south of Hollywood in the city of Anaheim.

The Orange and the Dream of California

Fruit of the Stars

The California Fruit Growers Exchange, which sold the dream of California while selling oranges, often incorporated motion picture stars into its Sunkist print and radio advertising. In 1940, it sponsored *Hedda Hopper's Hollywood* show, which ran three times a week on CBS stations across the country.

This publicity image for the 1927 film My Best Girl *shows Mary Pickford, one of the most popular and powerful stars in early Hollywood and affectionately dubbed "America's Sweetheart," drinking fresh-squeezed orange juice from an early Sunkist commercial juicer.*

In the late 1920s, when one-third of Americans attended the movies every day, Sunkist offered grocery store owners an easy way to attract their attention. Sunkist would send store owners a free set of large-format slides to be shown in theaters between films, featuring handsome images of California orange orchards along with the local grocer's name and address.

A 1931 wire service photo shows Mary Pickford, the first female movie mogul and one of the founders of the United Artists studio, with movie columnist Louella Parsons, "admiring Sunkist oranges."

The Orange and the Dream of California

MYRNA LOY, *beautiful star of Metro-Goldwyn-Mayer's "The Great Ziegfeld," tells you about the orange servings she likes best.*

Sunkist Salad Bowl
See page 23 of recipe booklet

Orange Ginger Ale
See page 28 of recipe booklet

Orange Charlotte
See page 33 of recipe booklet

Fruit Meal Salad
See page 23 of recipe booklet

FREE Recipe Book

"Here are my 4 favorite orange recipes" *Myrna Loy*

They're delicious and quickly made ...So why not try them all?

"IF you are as partial to oranges as I am, you know it isn't easy to choose your favorite ways to serve them! Of course, fresh orange juice would head any list so I won't count that.

"Next—the mixed salad bowl, with seasonal fruits and plenty of oranges. It is one of our most popular informal servings in California—often a first course!"

A "Whole Meal" Salad

"Another custom of ours is to plan a whole luncheon around a salad. So let's have one of that kind too.

"For dessert, my choice is Orange Charlotte. And my last is something to serve first—a cocktail for the thoughtful hostess to offer those who say 'No, thank you,' to other kinds!"

All of Miss Loy's favorites are in Sunkist's free recipe booklet. But you can make most of them from the illustrations—they are as simple as they are healthful.

How Oranges Aid Health

Oranges give you all four of the now-known protective food essentials that help keep you youthfully vigorous—vitamins C, A and B, and calcium.

They aid digestion also, and build the alkaline reserve in a natural way.

Two glasses of fresh orange juice, each with the juice of half a lemon, reduced gum troubles 83% and lessened tooth decay 57% in a 3¼-year research-study.

For your two glasses a day and for your recipes, be sure you get Sunkist California Oranges. The Valencias, now in season, are wonderfully sweet and juicy. Look for the name on the skin and tissue wrapper of *every* orange.

Free Recipe and Health Booklets with Safe Reducing Suggestions

Send coupon for the free booklet "Sunkist Recipes for Every Day," with more than 200 servings. Check if you also wish "Fruits That Help Keep the Body Vigorous." It explains the place of citrus fruits in the diet. Also how their high mineral and vitamin value and low calorie count help you "reduce" safely.

Copyright, 1936, California Fruit Growers Exchange

SUNKIST SENIOR EXTRACTOR
Fountains displaying it serve you real made-to-order fresh fruit drinks, with full value in vitamins and delicious flavor.

SUNKIST HAND EXTRACTOR
Glass. Scientific design. Millions sold. At department stores, 35c.

California Fruit Growers Exchange
Dept. 306, Sunkist Building
Los Angeles, California

( ) Send FREE, "Sunkist Recipes for Every Day."
( ) Send FREE, "Fruits That Help Keep the Body Vigorous."

Name_____
Street_____
City_____ State_____

Sunkist *Valencia* Oranges
FROM CALIFORNIA

June 1936 Good Housekeeping

Star of The Thin Man *series and many other films, Myrna Loy is featured in this 1936 magazine ad. "If you are as partial to oranges as I am, you know it isn't easy to choose your favorite ways to serve them!" she's quoted. The ad solves this dilemma by noting that "All of Miss Loy's favorites are in Sunkist's free recipe booklet."*

Ready for its Close-up—The Orange in Hollywood

MAGICAL TREE
of gold and white,
Fruit and blossoms
growing in sight,
Flowers of waxen
beauty rare,
Scenting the bridal maiden's
hair;
Glorious vision of life thou be,
CALIFORNIA'S ORANGE
TREE!

HECKER

486
COPYRIGHT 1913
P.F.VOLLAND & CO. Chicago, U.S.A.

This postcard, copyrighted 1913, was produced when the orange and California were celebrated across popular culture.

Words and Music—
Poems and Songs for California's Orange

With a name with which nothing rhymes
You know there are going to be times
When you might remain mute
When contemplating this fruit,
Even though it is so top-of-mind!

The couplets incessantly cheery, they do grow a little bit weary.
But it's refreshing to see that there's no irony,
The sentiments expressed, so sincere at their best,
It's clear that they loved the orange tree.

RHYMING WITH ORANGE

A romantic California ideal, complete with Roman-inspired ruins, eucalyptus trees, and oranges—all three elements imported to California from other parts of the world but woven into the California dream—decorates this 1930s greeting card. The verse inside includes "And the wish I keep repeating is that soon we may be meeting in the land of fruit and flowers."

"ORANGE" You ILL Long Enough?

Your friends ain't "SEED" you Much too long!
Oh golly, how they've missed you!

So, hope you'll soon Be UP and OUT--

It's time that old "SUN-KIST" You!

Greetings from California

DEAR . . . . . I WRITE TO LET YOU KNOW
THAT I AM FAR AWAY,
WHERE THERE IS NEITHER SLEET NOR SNOW
TO BOTHER ME TODAY.
THIS WEATHER IS THE BULLY KIND,
THIS TOWN'S A CRACKER JACK!
AND I HAVE JUST MADE UP MY MIND,
YOU'LL NEVER SEE ME BACK!

PRIVATE RESIDENCE

I'm Singing this Song for You

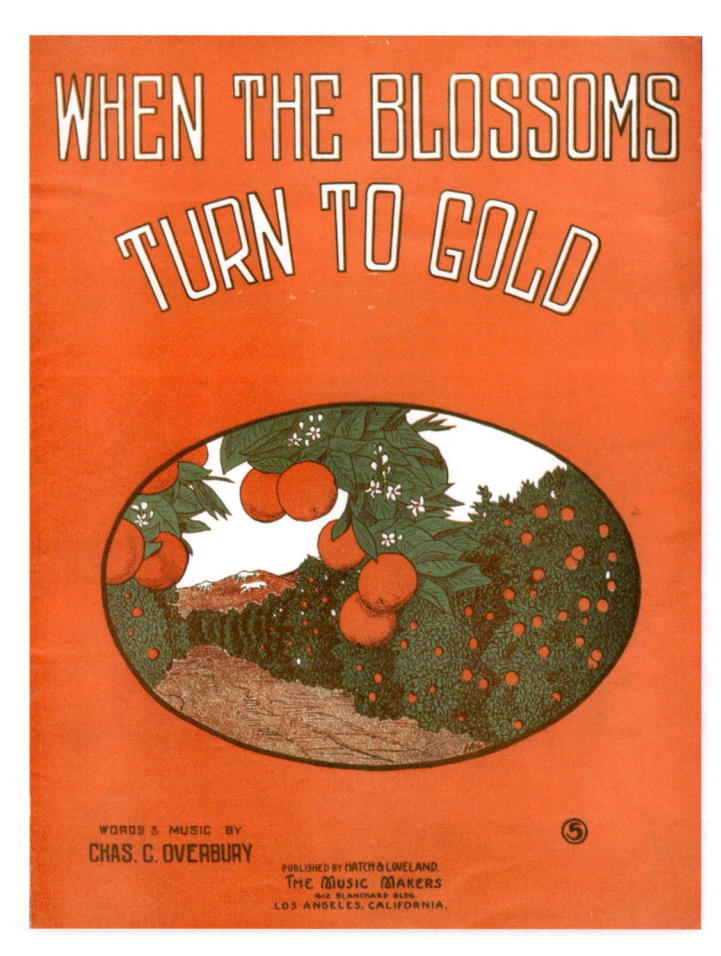

"In the land of golden promise where life's golden dreams come true,
there tonight my heart is resting and I'm dreaming, love, of you.
Thro' the groves once more we wander, in the blossom-scented breeze,
where the golden fruit is hanging with the blossoms on the trees."

"In California where the oranges grow,
I've found the place that I love best and built myself a cozy nest."

The Orange and the Dream of California

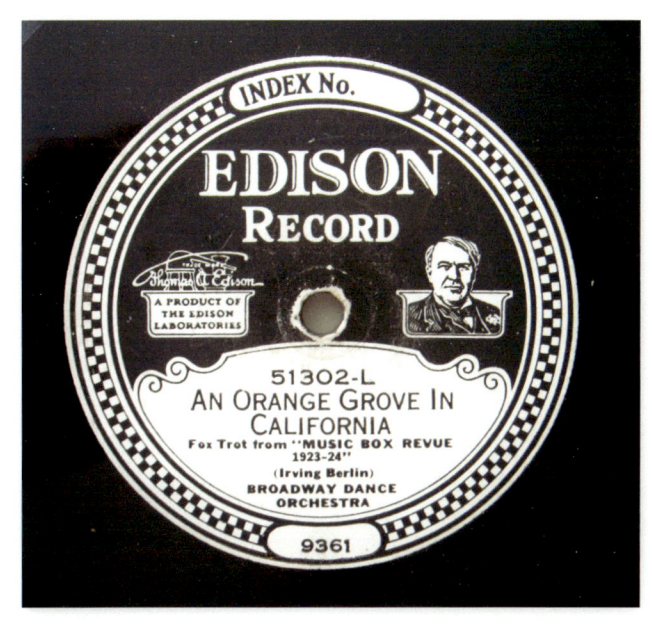

Written by Irving Berlin, An Orange Grove in California *was a hit in 1923, available in sheet music, as a record, and as a piano roll for use with a player piano. "Arm in arm we will rove thro' a sweet orange grove . . . When blossoms unfold and the green turns to gold."*

Words and Music—Poems and Songs for California's Orange

137

*"Sweet, sweet California, I hear you calling me.
My heart is yearning for your orange trees,
where all year 'round birds sing sweet melodies."*

*"It's orange blossom time and I'll cheer,
'cause I've got the ring and I hear those wedding chimes . . . "*

138

The Orange and the Dream of California

Orange Day in California

This song was commissioned for the March, 1916 Orange Day: "This day that we have set apart to feast on golden fruit, we hope that all our sister states will nobly follow suit. And in their hearts will thankful be for California's gift, and filled with praise for state and fruit, their voices to uplift. While in his native land, King Orange surely holds full sway, for here in California ev'ry day is orange day."

Words and Music—Poems and Songs for California's Orange

139

Enjoying California's charms, January, 1913.

10

Every Picture Tells a Story—
Snapshots of the Dream

*Expelled from the Garden of Eden and told that they would have to sweat it out
to make a living, humankind has turned that divine malediction
into what is arguably the most insistent Judeo-Christian mandate for a utopia:
find yourself a New World, go to the virgin lands,
and reap personal wealth and happiness along the way.*

PIERRE LASZLO
Citrus: A History, 2007

The photographs speak volumes. Thousands of casual photos—people standing by an orange tree, smiles beaming, arms reaching up, grasping a golden orange. In the distance, snowy mountains sparkle. The pictures say, "Look! I'm in California!! It's perfect!!!"

In 1906, Eastman Kodak Company began offering cameras that produced postcard-sized negatives, allowing anyone to create their own, one-of-a-kind postcards, and even caption them. This card, postmarked March 16, 1908, was sent from a niece in Orosi, California, to her uncle in Algona, Iowa.

"Where bowers of flowers bloom in the sun . . . Birdies sing an' everything.
A sun-kist miss said, 'Don't be late,' that's why I can hardly wait . . .
California here I come!"

AL JOLSON, BUD DE SYLVA, and JOSEPH MEYER
California Here I Come, 1921

Another Kodak postcard. On the back, in fountain-pen ink, is written, "This picture taken Feb. 5, 1912, at Ontario, California."

Many California photography studios set-up orange tree dioramas where tourists could have their portrait taken and get a California souvenir at the same time.

142   The Orange and the Dream of California

TOP: *Flag Studio, in Pasadena, was among those that offered an indoor orchard. These three images were taken in 1910, about a year after the studio was established. Flag offered customers tokens good for five cents off Kodak film.*
BOTTOM LEFT: *"I'll eat oranges for you, while you throw snowballs for me," was a popular California booster slogan. Here, amazed tourists do both. The photo is dated June 11, 1919.*
BOTTOM RIGHT: *Written on the back of this photograph: "Orange grove 25 miles southeast of Los Angeles, California, near Covina. Aug. 12, 1915, 5 p.m."*

Every Picture Tells a Story—Snapshots of the Dream

143

Top: *Paradise: a roadster, youth, and a beautiful California day.*
Bottom: *Is this Philip Marlowe? One would think yes, until reading what is written on the back of the photograph . . .*

A hard, unemployed, gray haired, worried, financially embarrased man-views a Calif. orange grove, while smoking his last cigarette! Now he builds Airplanes for C.A.C. Not bad, i hope!

144   The Orange and the Dream of California

"California is the world's paradigm of hope and opportunity."
JOHN JAKES
California Gold, 1980

Love the Band-Aids on both knees. Around the border of this photograph is written: "Robin, Anaheim, Cal., Dec., 1938."

This woman wrote on the back of this picture, "My share."

Every Picture Tells a Story—Snapshots of the Dream

California's golden oranges were not just an economic powerhouse; they were also a leading tourist attraction.

11

Tourists, Trolleys, and Trains

Southern California is by far the most beautiful and generally attractive section of country in the world.
MAJOR BEN C. TRUMAN, 1900

In 1862 there were about twenty-five thousand orange trees and fewer than a half a million people in California. With the arrival of the navel orange tree in 1873, the Southern Pacific Railroad in 1876, and the Santa Fe Railroad in 1885, the numbers of both grew at an astounding rate. Trainloads of oranges went east and returned with people, who came to see, then to stay.

To encourage tourism and investment, the Southern Pacific brought out *New York Evening Post* editor Charles Nordhoff who, inspired, wrote the best seller, *California for Health, Pleasure and Residence, A Book for Travelers and Settlers*. With the spirit of a true believer and the eager language of the era, he penned: "California . . . there and only there, on this planet, the traveler and resident may enjoy the delights of the tropics, without their penalties; a mild climate, not enervating, but healthful and health-restoring; a wonderfully and vigorously productive soil." Nordoff was joined by chambers of commerce, developers, health authorities, hotel owners—but especially the railroads—all gushing with superlatives about California and the promise of the orange. California was the Promised Land with "new waves of immigrants, primarily of the professional class, and many of them wealthy." Towns were established along the railroad routes, orchards were planted, and a series of land booms, with the requisite busts, were the result.

Towns, tourists, and trees were growing in California, and the automobile and efficient public transportation were also coming of age. The Pacific Electric

*When you come to consider the life that is encountered here,
you have to admit that there is a great deal to be said for it.*
James M. Cain
"Paradise," *The American Mercury*, 1933

Railway, or Red Car, was the largest interurban electric railway passenger service in the world in the early twentieth century. Residents and tourists could travel on over a thousand miles of track from downtown Los Angeles east to the San Fernando Valley, west as far as Redlands, and south to Newport Beach in Orange County.

And as the car transitioned from a plaything of the rich to reliable and affordable transportation for many—and as roads improved—the Sunday drive and family excursion became popular pastimes. Travel agencies and tour businesses thrived, offering both tourists and southern California residents maps, itineraries, and help with reservations. A 1926 travel guide promised: "You will find wonderfully paved highways radiating every direction, smooth and inviting. . . . You may . . . travel effortless mile after mile without ever getting off the pavement." It also assured that "automotive service of every needed character is available" and that "the tourist is 'given a square deal.'" Comforting information then as now.

This 1928 Los Angeles Chamber of Commerce ad appeared in National Geographic. *"From the balmy spring-like 'winter' sunshine of Southern California comes better health, renewed energy . . . happier living conditions." A life among the oranges drew millions to California.*

*One orange every day, freshly squeezed, will clear up the complexion in one week.
By the end of two weeks, your insecurities will be gone;
you'll be getting dates and going to parties.*
Karen Tei Yamashita
Tropic of Orange, 1997

148   The Orange and the Dream of California

Railroads do not eat oranges.
But America could not eat its oranges without railroads.
Santa Fe Railroad advertisement promoting its importance to the California citrus industry

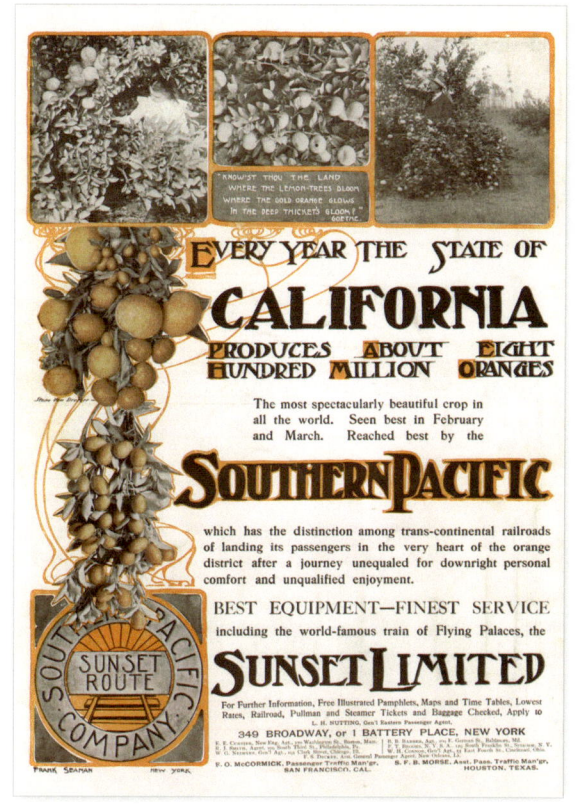

Tourists, Trolleys, and Trains

149

TOP: *An inscription on the back of a postcard mailed July 14, 1928: "Riding along in the train from Los Angeles to San Diego, how beautiful the orange groves look on both sides of the train."*

BOTTOM: *In the early 1900s, few paved roads and the still-experimental nature of the automobile made excursions like this an adventure only for the hearty and wealthy. The car in the foreground of this postcard is a Tourist, manufactured in Los Angeles by the Auto Vehicle Company between 1902 and 1910. The company's slogan was "Best in the Long Run."*

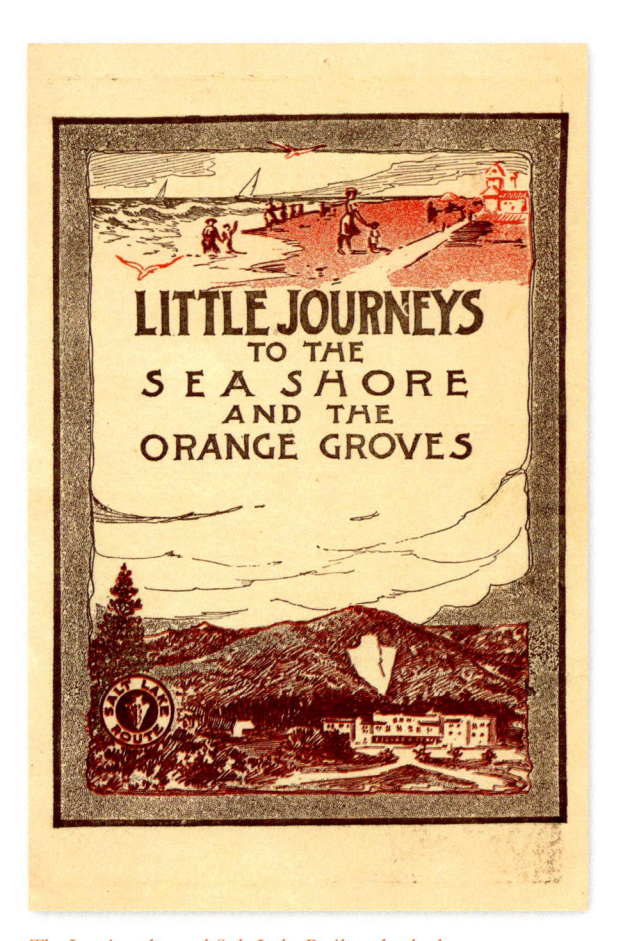

The Los Angeles and Salt Lake Railroad, also known as the Salt Lake Route, began service in 1905. Many of its depot buildings were designed in the Mission Revival style, which was popular and promoted a romanticized California past. "The most beautiful trip in Southern California is that through the great orange district . . . first stopping at a wonderful example of California's possibilities . . . Thirty years from desert to its present condition, [Riverside is] a beautiful city surrounded by orange groves." The LA&SL was taken over by Union Pacific in 1921.

The Orange and the Dream of California

Before freeways there was the Pacific Electric Railway, which ran almost everywhere including sightseeing excursions "to the heart of the world's greatest Orange Empire . . . (See) scenes of verdure, realms of productiveness and vistas of beauty that only in California can man's hand create" promised a brochure.

Tourists, Trolleys, and Trains

151

HERBERT'S FAMOUS ORANGE TOURS---FREE

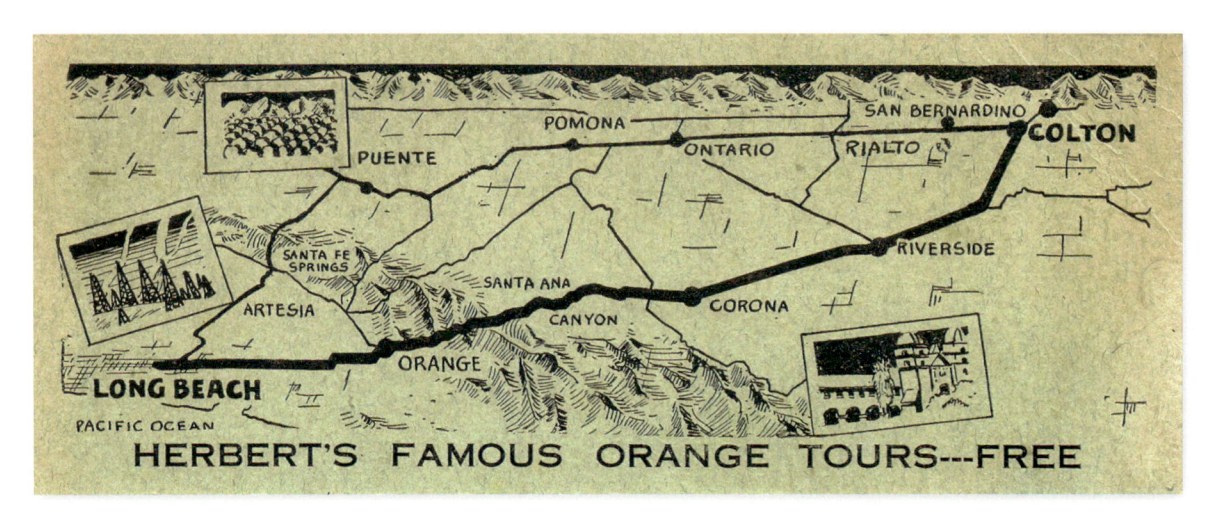

"See the real California you have dreamed about, and heard in song and story," claimed a tour company based in Long Beach, California, and many miles from the Orange Belt. "A Tour Worth While," it boasted, and offered as an extra enticement, "Have a hot country dinner among the orange trees."

This travel guide was produced for the California motoring tourist in 1926.

Well into the 1950s oranges were still a California tourist draw, although the text in this ad from Holiday *magazine—sponsored by the Los Angeles County Board of Supervisors—also promoted Hollywood and the "new steel and glass Civic Center." Times were changing.*

152

The Orange and the Dream of California

A giant orange is something to seek out.
GLORIA SCOTT, architectural historian

JUST ANOTHER ROADSIDE ATTRACTION— HIGHWAY ORANGE JUICE STANDS

At a time when the only automobile air-conditioning available consisted of rolling down the windows, traveling California's vast and warm central valley could be a thirsty experience. Spotting a refreshment stand in the shape of a giant orange was a welcome and somewhat magical sight.

The first Giant Orange stand was built by Frank and Lora Pohl in the northern California town of Tracy in 1926. The Pohls, like many others at the time, realized that as automobiles became capable of traveling faster and further, shaping their establishment to represent what it sold was a way to grab the attention of speeding drivers. There were eventually more than a dozen Giant Orange stands, and they were joined by competitors like Orange Basket, Great Orange, Big Boy Orange, Mammoth Orange, The Orange, Whoa Boy Orange, Big Orange, and George's Orange.

Whimsical orange stands dotted California's Highway 99, a major north-south thoroughfare. Travelers could stretch their legs, get a bite to eat and grab a bag of oranges for the road.

Tourists, Trolleys, and Trains

Like lunch counters and soda fountains across the country, California's orange-shaped roadside stands provided customers fresh-squeezed California sunshine from commercial extractors sold by Sunkist—at cost—to encourage the drinking of orange juice.

Love as big as an orange.

The Orange and the Dream of California

*"The Giant Orange stands evoked a sense of roadside security to weary, wandering motorists,"
explained Patricia Buckley in her charming history of these establishments, Those Unforgettable Giant Oranges (1987).
A refreshing glass of hand-squeezed OJ cost fifteen cents.*

Tourists, Trolleys, and Trains

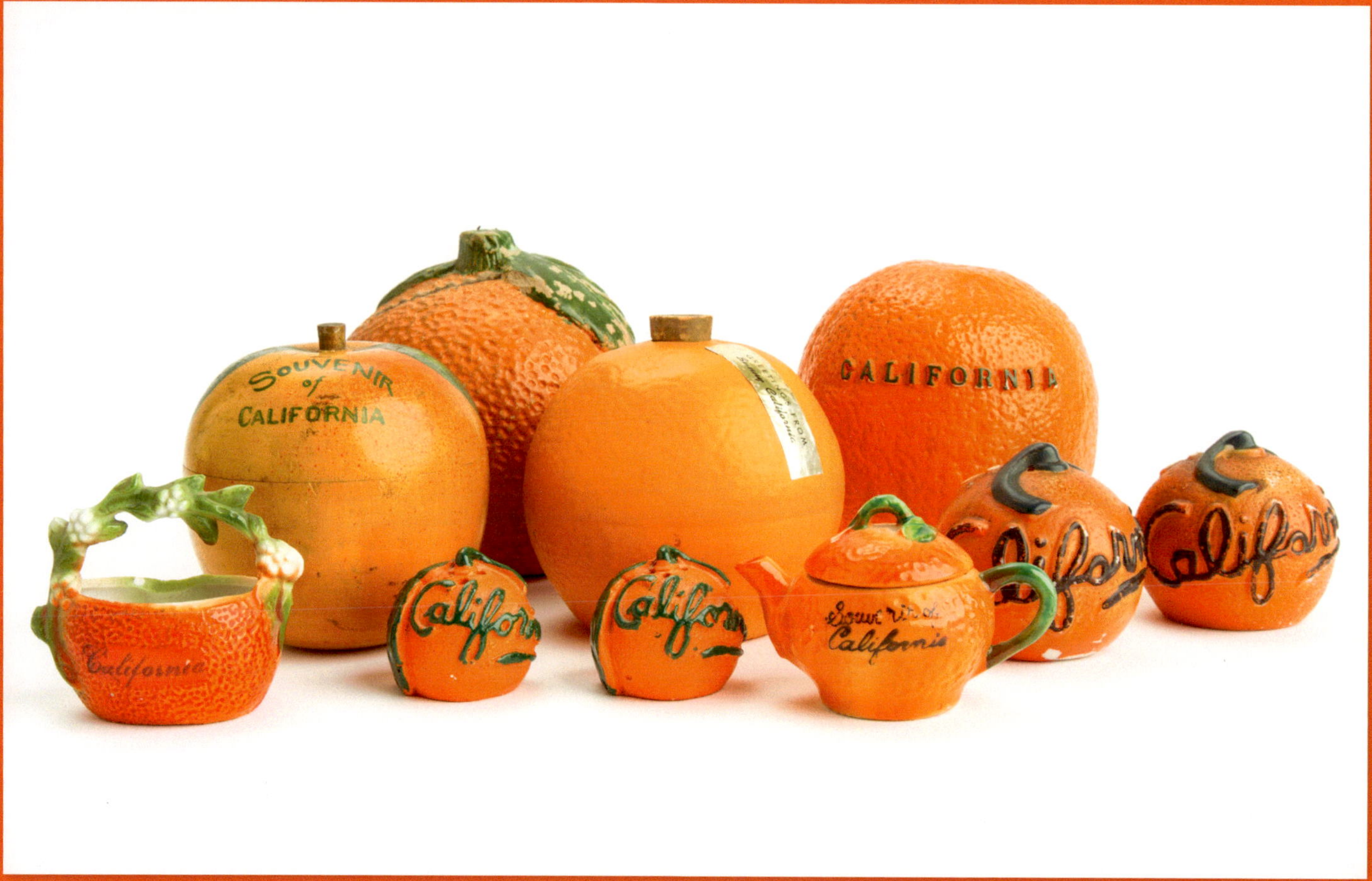
SOUVENIR
of
CALIFORNIA
CALIFORNIA
California

12

A Little Bit of Paradise for the Folks Back Home— California Orange Souvenirs

For the most part, the audience of the earlier age eagerly grasped at the glittering dreams so beautifully conceived and so well-spun in booster ephemera. These throw-away items, produced by the thousands, represented more than . . . new jobs, new homes and a tourist destination. The elements of boosterism, hyperbole and romanticized graphics can be dismissed as the glitter of fool's gold . . . but the words and images had great impact on all that the state has become since, and far exceeded the wildest predictions of those who created the golden dreams.

K.D. KURUTZ and GARY F. KURUTZ
California Calls You: The Art of Promoting the Golden State 1870 to 1940, 2000

The California State Library has an extraordinary collection of elegantly rendered, fabulously conceived print materials from the golden age of California promotion. The imagination and artistry used in presenting the real and make-believe charms of California is astonishing. No less captivating than those beautiful depictions, however, the objects presented here are equally evocative, if considerably less high-concept. Some are just wacky. But these simple souvenirs played a role, too, in presenting California as a place of dreams.

Distributed by Duvinne of New York beginning in the 1920s, this divided glass globe contained three small vials of perfume "suggestive of the blossom scented breezes from the orange groves." Enclosed in the box of this example was a handwritten note dated March 3, 1942, saying "From Aunt Millie to Irene." Based on its remarkable condition, it is likely the globe had never been removed from the box until this photo was taken.

This character, Ozzie Orange, was originally created for the Pure Gold brand, and was one of three anthropomorphic citrus personalities unveiled at a 1930s industry banquet. The others were Pedro Pomelo and Lily Lemon.

158   The Orange and the Dream of California

TOP LEFT: *Invented by Sir Charles Wheatstone in 1838, stereoscopy creates the illusion of depth in an image by slightly offsetting two identical images and fooling the brain. Stereopticon viewers were popular entertainment in late-nineteenth and early-twentieth centuries, and many thousands of different subjects were offered, including many showing the California orange empire.*

RIGHT: *Stereopticon viewers were enjoyed around the world; some cards came with captions in six languages and additional explanatory text on the back. An excerpt from one card: "This is one of the most famous garden-lands in the world, and it has actually been created by human skill out of a sun-baked plain in Southern California since 1870."*

Some cards were hand colored, like this one from 1897.

A Little Bit of Paradise for the Folks Back Home

159

A decal like this on the window of the family station wagon or travel trailer let everyone know you'd been to the land of sunshine and oranges.

The Orange and the Dream of California

Miniature orange crates, complete with fanciful crate labels, were filled with orange candy. When addressed right on the crate or the attached tag, they could be mailed anywhere in the U.S. for three cents.

"Orange Blossom" pattern dinnerware was produced by California Ceramics Company in the 1940s and '50s, and sold under the names Orchard Ware and Hollywood Ware.

A Little Bit of Paradise for the Folks Back Home

161

162   The Orange and the Dream of California

Stamps of Approval

Gummed and perforated like postage stamps, but usually slightly larger, poster stamps became popular in the mid-1800s. They were used for advertising and promotion of political and philanthropic causes and were widely collected into the 1930s.

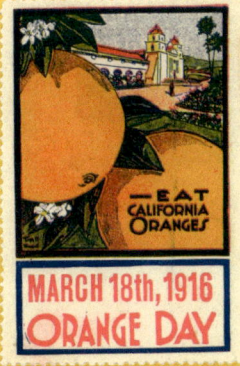

Orange Day was promoted by the citrus industry and officially by the State of California. The artwork on these stamps was also used in advertising, postcards, and on sheet music.

A Little Bit of Paradise for the Folks Back Home

163

As much of California was turning from citrus production to industrialization and tract housing, Weldon Field of Orange County was in high demand, using his self-designed and -built "stump puller" to clear away what had been for decades at the core of the state's prosperity and identity.

13

Paradise Lost—From Land of Enchantment to Suburban Plenty

*The very things that made it an idyllic land were what attracted
the multitudes who were to make it into a sprawling, shrouded metropolis...
Paradise lost can never be regained.*

LAWRENCE CLARK POWELL
An Orange Grove Boyhood, 1988

The dream of California has been that it is a place of plenty, of potential, of personal opportunity. Its weather, resources, and spirit have drawn people who wanted to create a better life for themselves. The realities of the place—along with extravagant promotion—promised new beginnings, new wealth, and a healthier and more fulfilling life. The orange was the symbol of this dream.

The Orange Empire lasted about a century. Like many other empires before, circumstances beyond its control forced its collapse. World War II brought the end of King Citrus. It offered millions of GIs a chance to see the marvels of California as they cycled through it on their way to and from war; a great many of them came back to live in the state when the fighting was over. The war also cemented California's place at the center of the aerospace industry and jump-started other industrial development. The result was a historic

From my viewpoint, by the 1950s, the good ol' days were gone . . .
RUTH BRYCE
Quoted in *Beyond the Harvest: the History of the Fillmore Citrus Association*, 1997

explosion of population, housing, and building. A few numbers:

- Between 1940 and 1950, California's population grew from 6.9 to 10.6 million, 54 percent.
- In a single day in 1946, 107 houses were sold in the newly created city of Lakewood, California.
- In 2013, California agricultural land was being converted to industrial use, highways, shopping centers, schools, and housing at a rate of twenty thousand acres a year.

Political cartoonist Ted Rall has labeled similar seismic changes as the "disintegration threatening the appeal of the California dream."[40] It's hard to say. The place still has a lot going for it.

California has more than eight hundred miles of coastline with some of the best weather on the planet; the variety and beauty of the state's landscape remains unparalleled. California has tons of political influence; Silicon Valley; one of the most culturally diverse and talented populations anywhere; and if it were a nation, it would have the world's eighth-largest economy. The people who were drawn to try their hands at citriculture had a tremendous influence on California and its image. They combined high-mindedness with ambition, conformity with eccentricity. The state continues to draw these types of people, people looking for "a place where human beings might break through the constraints of day-to-day life and come into possession of something immeasurably better."[41] California's future may be bright, perhaps brighter than ever.

But what of its orange? California still produces almost a hundred million cartons of navels a year. However, grown in an out-of-the-way area nestled against the Sierra Nevada Mountains, the orchards are not tourist attractions, don't rival any of the state's top revenue generators, and are not symbolic of anything—except, maybe, that all things must pass. In 1870, a California grower said, "People tell large stories about oranges, but the truth is big enough." That truth shaped California in ways significant and frivolous, and the orange became and continues to be a beautiful, tasty, healthy symbol of both the fantasy and substance of the California Dream.

While massive change was coming soon, a commemorative postage stamp marked California's state centennial in 1950. The stamp shows the Golden State's three icons—the Gold Rush, oil, and oranges—not the movies, not aerospace, not its renowned universities, nor its freeways, and not yet, of course, its Silicon Valley.

The Orange and the Dream of California

*Leaders long ago deemed bark-and-leaf orange groves worthless.
And yet, as an abstraction, as propaganda, as a symbol of our civic ambition,
King Citrus reigns as powerful as ever . . . those pastorals function
as historical documents, primary sources of a past that never existed.*

GUSTAVO ARELLANO
Los Angeles Times, 2008

Established in 1913, the North Whittier Heights Citrus Association shuttered its packinghouse in August, 1960. It was the last of twelve such organizations in that immediate area. Citing low yields due to "decreased orchard care, and subdivision" as the reasons for closing, this one association over its forty year existence had produced crops valued at over fifty-two million dollars.

Empire Falls. One of California's oldest, unaltered, surviving orange groves, located in Orange County, might yet become another housing tract. A well-organized group, however, is fighting to take control of the property, which has two hundred and fifty orange trees and its original 1913 farmhouse. The Old Orchard Conservancy's dream is to use the restored orchard and house as a community education and culture center, celebrating the area's agricultural history and heritage.

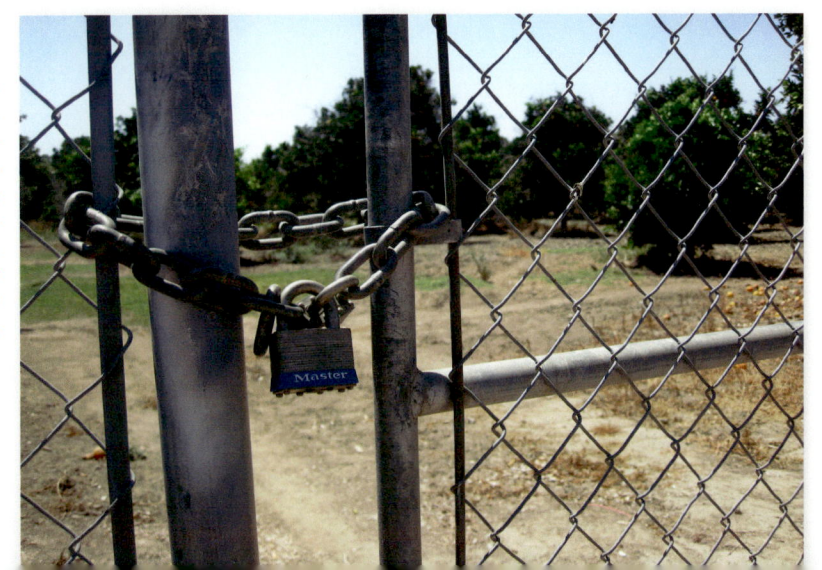

Paradise Lost

167

*The orange grove is lovely at all times.
It has a mysterious air when the long alleys
are dark against the red of sunset.
At twilight the fruit glimmers on its boughs like
a feast of lanterns not yet fully lighted.
In the free pleasant mornings we watch the sparkle
of the yellow globes among the glossy dark leaves,
and catch, perhaps, the perfume
of some few blossoms heralding in
a new crop while the last still hangs.*

WILLIAM HENRY BISHOP
Harper's Magazine, 1882

NOTES

1. Reuther, *The Citrus Industry,* Vol. I. (1967), 1.
2. Ibid, 190.
3. Laszlo, *Citrus: A History,* 10.
4. Gallesio, *Traité du Citrus,* 302-303. Quoted in Reuther, *The Citrus Industry,* Vol. I. (1967), 10-11.
5. Ferrari, *Hesperides,* 480. Quoted in Reuther, *The Citrus Industry,* Vol. I. (1967), 11.
6. Fenton, *A Place in the Sun.* Quoted in McWilliams, *Southern California,* 227.
7. Starr, *California,* 75.
8. Hughes, *The California of the Padres,* 35.
9. Spalding, *The Orange,* 2.
10. Wickson, *California Garden-Flowers,* 7.
11. Starr, *California,* 15.
12. Jackson, *The Indian Reform Letters,* 298.
13. McWilliams, *California,* 3.
14. Maynard, "The Story of the Seedless Orange," 25.
15. Liebeck, "The Life of William Wolfskill. Part II" 18.
16. Merlo, *Heritage of Gold,* 4.
17. Quoted in Brown, *San Bernardino,* 73.
18. Starr, *Inventing the Dream,* 46.
19. Ibid, 139.
20. Truman, *Oranges & Snowfields.*
21. Quoted in Ortlieb and Economy, *Creating an Orange Utopia,* 47.
22. Quoted in McWilliams, *Southern California,* 75.
23. Coit, *Citrus Fruits,* 10.
24. Brown and Boyd, *San Bernardino,* 74.
25. Ibid, 430.
26. Klotz, *History of Citrus,* 298.
27. Merlo and Peters, *Heritage of Gold,* 10.
28. Hanney, "Sun Kissed."
29. Ibid.
30. Merlo and Peters, *Heritage of Gold,* 46.
31. Lazlo, *Citrus, A History,* 114.
32. Blythe, "California Citrus," 39.
33. Starr, *Inventing,* 161.
34. Brown and Boyd, *San Bernardino,* 80.
35. Starr, *California,* xii.
36. Reuther, *The Citrus Industry,* Vol. V. (1967), 284.
37. Ibid, 291.
38. Ortlieb and Economy, *Creating an Orange Utopia,* 90.
39. Gonzalez, "Women, Work, and Community," 62.
40. Rall, "A Year in Cartoons," A30.
41. Starr, *California,* xi.

BIBLIOGRAPHY

Research in the twenty-first century has been given a great boost with the ever-expanding material available through the Internet—not as a replacement for primary source investigation, or as a substitute for what can be learned from holding an actual object in one's hands—but because it puts so much access and detail at a writer's fingertips. I specifically want to commend Google Books, Google Images, the Internet Archive, and Wikipedia. These sites provided rapid verification of minor details too numerous to list here, as well as leads to other sources. Among the subject areas where Wikipedia was particularly helpful with specifics were Jean Eugene Robert-Houdin, Max Weber, postcards, A.C. Gilbert Company, and the Pacific Electric Railway.

Adamic, Louis. *The Truth about Los Angeles*. Little Blue Book, No. 647. Girard, Kansas: Haldeman-Julius Publications, 1927.

Arellano, Gustavo. "Gunkist Oranges." *Orange County Weekly*, June 8, 2006. http://www.ocweekly.com/2006-06-08/news/gunkist-oranges/full/.

———. "Orange County's Lost Essence." *Los Angeles Times*, August 10, 2008, Opinion Sec.

Barron, Hal S. "Citriculture and Southern California: New Historical Perspectives." *California History* 74, no. 1 (Spring 1995): 2-5.

Bell, Alison. "Southern California's Great Citrus Had Its Crate Advertising." *Los Angeles Times*, April 27, 2011, sec. A.

Bennett, John E. "Roofing Over Orange Orchards in Southern California." *Harper's Weekly*, January 6, 1900, 22.

Bishop, William Henry. "Southern California. III.–From the Tehachapi Pass to the Mexican Frontier." *Harper's Magazine* 66, no. 391 (December 1882): 45-65.

Blythe, Stuart O. "California Citrus: Sunkist Growers Set the Pace for a Great American Industry." *Californiia : Magazine of Pacific Business*, February 1937, 11.

Brook, Harry Ellington. *Land of Sunshine: Southern California : An Authentic Description of Its Natural Features, Resources and Prospects*. Los Angeles: World's Fair Association and Bureau of Information Print, 1893.

Brown, Enos. "The Orange in Northern California." *Scientific American* 88, no. 8 (February 21, 1903): 138-39.

Brown, John, Jr., and James Boyd. *San Bernardino and Riverside Counties: With Selected Biography of Actors and Witnesses of the Period of Growth and Achievement*. Vol. 1. Chicago: Lewis Publishing Company, 1922.

Buckley, Patricia R. *Those Unforgettable Giant Oranges*. [Self-published] 1987.

Burchell, Sidney Herbert. *Jacob Peek, Orange Grower: A Tale of Southern California*. London: Gay and Hancock, 1915.

Cain, James M. "Paradise." *American Mercury* 66, No. 391 (March 1933). [Reprinted at http://www.latimes.com/entertainment/news/books/la-ca-cain-essay-20120101,0,3803540,full.story]

"California Fruit Growers Exchange." In *Advertising Case History*. Portfolio 7. Philadelphia: Curtis Pub., 1947.

Chandler, Raymond. *The Big Sleep*. New York: Alfred A. Knopf, 1939.

Coit, John Eliot. *Citrus Fruits: An Account of the Citrus Industry with Special Reference to California Requirements and Practices and Similar Conditions*. New York: Macmillan Company, 1915.

Evening Herald. "Orange Show Spirit Holds Citrus Belt in Its Grasp." February 19, 1912.

Fenton, Frank. *A Place in the Sun*. New York: Random House, 1942.

Ferrari, Giovanni Battista. *Hesperides Sive De Malorum Aureorum Cultura Et Usu Libri Quatuor Io. Baptistae Ferrarii Senensis*. Romae: Scheus, 1646.

"The Food Machinery Corporation (FMC) Photograph Collection," Riverside Public Library. http://www.riversideca.gov/library/history_aids_fmc.asp.

Francisco, Don. Papers. Special Collections Research Center, Syracuse University Libraries .

G. Harold Powell : Memorial. [Los Angeles], 1922. [Internet Archive: http://archive.org/stream/gharoldpowellmem00losaiala#page/n1/mode/2up]

Gallesio, Georges. *Traité Du Citrus.* Paris: Louis Fantin, 1811.

Garey, Thomas A., and L. J. Rose. *Orange Culture in California.* San Francisco: Pub. for A.T. Garey, Printed and Sold at the Office of the Pacific Rural Press, 1882.

Gonzalez, Gilbert. "Women, Work, and Community in the Mexican *Colonias* of the Southern California Citrus Belt." *California History* 74, No. 1 (Spring 1995): 58-67.

Grandin, Greg. *Fordlandia: The Rise and Fall of Henry Ford's Forgotten Jungle City.* New York: Metropolitan Books, 2009.

Groves, Martha. "California's Main Squeeze : Orange-shaped Juice Stands Recall State's Simpler Days." *Los Angeles Times*, March 3, 2010, AA sec.

Hanlin, Russ, Jr. "The Bridge from Uncultivated to Urban." Speech, Exhibit Opening Pasadena Museum of History, November 15, 2005.

Hanney, Delores. "Sun Kissed." Unpublished Manuscript, 2009. Typewritten.

Hartig, Anthea M. "In a World He Has Created: Class Collectivity and the Growers' Landscape of the Southern California Citrus Industry, 1890-1940." *California History* 74, No. 1 (Spring 1995): 100-11.

Hawthorne, Christopher. "Reading L.A.: Louis Adamic and Morrow Mayo," Review of *The Truth About Los Angeles*, by Louis Adamic and *Los Angeles*, by Morrow Mayo. *Los Angeles Times*, January 31, 2011.

"Horticulture vs. Manufacturing." *Land of Sunshine*, June 1894, 11.

Hughes, Elizabeth. *The California of the Padres; Or, Footprints of Ancient Communism.* San Francisco: I.N. Choynski, 1875.

Jackson, Helen Hunt. *The Indian Reform Letters of Helen Hunt Jackson, 1879-1885.* Edited by Valerie Sherer Mathes. Norman, Oklahoma: University of Oklahoma Press, 1998.

Jakes, John. *California Gold: A Novel.* New York: Random House, 1989.

James, George Wharton. *Heroes of California; the Story of the Founders of the Golden State as Narrated by Themselves or Gleaned from Other Sources,.* Boston: Little, Brown, 1910.

——. "The Romance of a Mountain." *Out West*, May 1913, 257-67.

Katz, Ephraim. *The Film Encyclopedia.* New York: HarperCollins Publishers, 1994.

Klotz, Esther, Harry W. Lawton, and Joan H. Hall. *A History of Citrus in the Riverside Area.* Revised ed. Riverside, California: Riverside Museum Press, 1969.

Kurutz, K. D., and Gary F. Kurutz. *California Calls You: The Art of Promoting the Golden State, 1870 to 1940.* Sausalito, California: Windgate Press, 2000.

Larsen, Grace H. "Commentary: The Economics and Structure of the Citrus Industry: Comment on Papers by H. Vincent Moses and Ronald Tobey and Charles Wetherell." *California History* 74, no. 1 (Spring 1995): 38-45.

Laszlo, Pierre. *Citrus: A History.* Chicago: University of Chicago Press, 2007.

Liebeck, Judy Gauntt. "The Life of William Wolfskill." Pts. I and II. *Citrograph*, (January/February 2011): 19-21; (March/April 2011): 19-22.

Lobdell, William. "Eviction Is Bitter Fruit of Citrus Man's Labors." *Los Angeles Times*, June 15, 2008, California sec.

Lummis, Charles Fletcher. "The Right Hand of the Continent [Part IV]." *Out West* 8, No. 4 (April 1903): 415-31.

MacCurdy, Rahno Mabel. *The History of the California Fruit Growers Exchange.* Los Angeles: [G. Rice & Sons], 1925.

Mack, Robert Angus. "Rain-Making for the Orange Grower." *Technical World Magazine* 21 (July 1912).

Marcum, Diana. "Mammoth Orange Food Stand Suddenly a Hot Commodity." *Los Angeles Times*, June 3, 2012, Local sec.

Maynard, LaSalle A. "The Story of the Seedless Orange." *The World To-Day*, January 1907, 25-32.

Mayo, Morrow. *Los Angeles*. New York: Alfred A. Knopf, 1933.

McBane, Margo. "The Role of Gender in Citrus Employment: A Case Study of Recruitment, Labor, and Housing Patterns at the Limoneira Company, 1893 to 1940." *California History* 74, no. 1 (Spring 1995): 68-81.

McCarthy, John Russell. "The 'Golden Apple' Goes West." *California History Nugget* 7, no. 5 (February 1940): 131-37.

McClelland, Gordon, and Jay T. Last. *California Orange Box Labels: An Illustrated History*. Beverly Hills, California: Hillcrest Press, 1985.

McPhee, John. *Oranges*. New York: Farrar, Straus and Giroux, 1967.

McWilliams, Carey. *California: The Great Exception*. Westport, CT: Greenwood Press, 1971. [First California Paperback Printing: Berkeley: University of California Press, 1998.]

——. *Southern California: An Island on the Land*. Layton, Utah: Gibbs Smith, 1973.

Merlo, Catherine. *Beyond the Harvest: The History of the Fillmore-Piru Citrus Association : 1897-1997*. Fillmore, California: Fillmore-Piru Citrus Association, 1997.

Merlo, Catherine, and Claire H. Peters. *Heritage of Gold: The First 100 Years of Sunkist Growers, Inc., 1893-1993*. Sherman Oaks, CA: Sunkist Growers, 1994.

Moses, H. Vincent. "The Orange-Grower Is Not a Farmer: G. Harold Powell, Riverside Orchardists, and the Coming of Industrial Agriculture, 1893-1930." *California History* 74, no. 1 (Spring 1995): 22-37.

Naftzger, A. H. "Marketing California Oranges and Lemons." *The Land of Sunshine. : The Magazine of California and the West* 14 (1901): 247-252.

Nason, Frank Lewis. *The Vision of Elijah Berl*. Boston: Little, Brown, 1905.

Nordhoff, Charles. *California: For Health, Pleasure, and Residence : A Book for Travellers and Settlers*. New York: Harper & Brothers, 1873.

"Orange Culture in California." *Scientific American* 88, no. 25 (June 20, 1903): 466.

"Orange Growing." *Land of Sunshine*, July 1894, 33.

Ortlieb, Patricia, and Peter Economy. *Creating an Orange Utopia: Eliza Lovell Tibbets & the Birth of California's Citrus Industry*. West Chester, Pennsylvania: Swedenborg Foundation Press, 2011.

Pennoyer, Albert Sheldon, ed. *This Was California; a Collection of Woodcuts and Engravings Reminiscent of Historical Events, Human Achievements and Trivialities from Pioneer Days to the Gay Nineties,*. New York: G.P. Putnam's Sons, 1938.

Powell, George Harold. *Letters from the Orange Empire*. Edited by Richard Gordon Lillard. Los Angeles: Historical Society of Southern California, 1990.

Powell, Lawrence Clark. *An Orange Grove Boyhood: Growing up in Southern California, 1910-1928*. Santa Barbara: Capra Press, 1988.

Price, Steven D. *1001 Greatest Things Ever Said about California*. Guilford, Connecticut: Lyons Press, 2007.

Rall, Ted. "A Year in Cartoons." *Los Angeles Times*, December 30, 2012.

Reuther, Walter, and Herbert John Webber. *The Citrus Industry*. Rev. Ed. [Berkeley]: University of California, Division of Agricultural Sciences, 1967. v. 1: *History, World Distribution, Botany, and Varieties* /edited by Walter Reuther, Herbert John Webber, Leon Dexter Batchelor ; with the Collaboration of J. Henry Burke ... [et Al.] — v. 5: *Crop Protection, Postharvest Technology, and Early History of Citrus Research in California* / Edited by Walter Reuther, E. Clair Calavan, Glen E. Carman Collaboration of Lee R. Jepson ... [et Al.].

Rizzo, Tania. "The Flag Collection." *Pasadena Muuseum of History Newsletter*, Spring 2000, 4.

Rolle, Andrew F., and Arthur Verge. *California; a History*. 7th ed. Wheeling, Illinois: Harlan Davidson, 2008.

Sackman, Douglas Cazaux. "By Their Fruits Ye Shall Know Them: 'Nature Cross Culture Hybridization' and the California Citrus Industry, 1893-1939." *California History* 74, No. 1 (Spring 1995): 82-99.

———. *Orange Empire: California and the Fruits of Eden*. Berkeley: University of California Press, 2005.

Salkin, John, and Laurie Gordon. *Orange Crate Art*. New York: Warner Books, 1976.

Smith, Bertha H. "The Making of Los Angeles: A Study of the Astonishing Growth of California's Southland City—Oranges, Palms and Fast-Rising Sky-Scrapers—Present Population Close to 300,000." *Sunset* 19 (1907): 237-54.

Southern California: Comprising the Counties of Imperial, Los Angeles, Orange, Riverside, San Bernardino, San Diego, Ventura;. [San Diego?]: Southern California Panama Expositions Commission, 1914.

Spalding, William Andrew. *The Orange : Its Culture in California: With a Brief Discussion of the Lemon, Lime, and Other Citrus Fruits*. Riverside, California: Press and Horticulturist Steam Print., 1885.

Spellman, Tom. "Artists of the Era." *Citrograph*, July/August 2011, 21-23.

———. "The Citrus Label Era (1887-1955)." *Citrograph*, July/August 2011, 21-22.

Starr, Kevin. *Americans and the California Dream, 1850-1915*. New York: Oxford University Press, 1973.

———. *California: A History*. New York: Modern Library, 2005.

———. *Inventing the Dream: California through the Progressive Era*. New York: Oxford University Press, 1985.

"State Honors First Navel Orange Tree." *California Highways and Public Works*, March 1933, 21. [Reprinted at http://libraryarchives.metro.net/DPGTL/Californiahighways/chpw_1933_mar.pdf.]

Steiner, Michael C. "Commentary: Reading the Citrus Landscape: Comments concerning Papers by Douglas Sackman and Anthea Hartig." *California History* 74, no. 1 (Spring 1995): 112-17.

Sutherland, Allan. "Orange Culture in California." *The Booklovers Magazine* 3, No. 6 (June 1904): 803-11.

Teague, Charles Collins. *Fifty Years a Rancher: The Recollections of Half a Century Devoted to the Citrus and Walnut Industries of California and to Furthering the Cooperative Movement in Agriculture*. 2nd ed. Los Angeles: Ward Ritchie Press, 1944.

Tobey, Ronald, and Charles Wetherell. "The Citrus Industry and the Revolution of Corporate Capitalism in Southern California, 1887-1944." *California History* 74, no. 1 (Spring 1995): 6-21.

Truman, Benjamin Cummings. *Oranges & Snowfields: Southern California at the Turn of the Century*. Edited by Graham Mackintosh. Santa Barbara, California: Ross-Erikson, 1977.

Van Dyke, Theodore S. *Southern California: Its Valleys, Hills and Streams; Its Animals, Birds, and Fishes; Its Gardens, Farms and Climate*. New York: Fords, Howard & Hulbert, 1886.

Vaught, David. *Cultivating California: Growers, Specialty Crops, and Labor, 1875-1920*. Baltimore: Johns Hopkins University Press, 1999.

Wallschlaeger, F.O. "Citrus Food Industries of California." *California's Magazine ... a Quarterly Journal for the Dissemination of Authentic Information concerning California* 1 (July 1915): 447-60.

Weir, D.B. "A Modern Hesperides." *Californian Illustrated Magazine* 4, no. 3 (August 1893).

White, Timothy. *The Nearest Faraway Place: Brian Wilson, the Beach Boys, and the Southern California Experience*. New York: H. Holt, 1994.

Whittier News. "Last of Packing Houses to Close." August 25, 1960, sec. A.

Wickson, Edward J. *California Garden-flowers, Shrubs, Trees and Vines; Being Mainly Suggestions for Working Amateurs,*. San Francisco: Pacific Rural Press, 1915.

Wyman, Mark. *Hoboes: Bindlestiffs, Fruit Tramps, and the Harvesting of the West*. New York: Hill and Wang, 2010.

Yamashita, Karen Tei. *Tropic of Orange: A Novel*. Minneapolis: Coffee House Press, 1997.

Image Credits

Thanks to David Young-Wolff for photography of objects, including books, juicers, and souvenirs.

With these exceptions, all images are from the author's collection. Thanks to:
Anaheim Heritage Center, Anaheim Public Library: 84 (right).
Bridgeman Art Library: 12, 15 (left), 16 (top), 18.
Citrus Label Society: 104 (top row), 118 (top, bottom right), 119 (top right, bottom right), 120 (all).
Luis Garcia: 14.
Bill Hahn: 101 (all).
Jim Heimann: 153, 154 (right), 155.
The Huntington Library, San Marino, California: 55.
Los Angeles Public Library Photo Collection: 34 (all), 83 (left), 102 (left).
Joe Martinez: 16 (bottom), 19 (bottom).
Occidental College Library, Special Collections and College Archives: 47 (right).
Orange County Archives: 164.
Freer Gallery of Art, Smithsonian Institution, Washington, D.C.: 17.
Sunkist Growers, Inc.: 44, 45 (bottom left), 48, 50, 54, 62 (bottom left), 67 (top), 95, 113 (left), 117, 129.

University of Southern California Library, Department of Special Collections: 28.

Acknowledgments

This book evolved over a considerable period of time. The journey has been most excellent, and it was made possible by the encouragement, support, and generous time and energy of a great many people and institutions.

Starting at the beginning, thank you Jim Heimann for asking me—almost four decades ago—to ride the Amtrak with you to a San Diego paper ephemera show. While you worked to find scrap for an illustration project, I discovered a new world and bought my first two orange-themed postcards. Those cards were the start of my collection, my education, this book.

Several decades and hundreds of postcards later, Earl Beadle fed my mania by giving me a copy of John McPhee's wonderful Oranges. This piqued my interest in the facts behind the lovely images. Thank you, Earl.

Then, after still more years, and while listening to Dr. Kevin Starr speak at Occidental College, I was struck with idea that a personal fascination and individual zeal might create a collection that is more than a hobby or indulgence; that perhaps an interest in history and a focused assembling of materials would bring to light details and the discovery of connections others had not. With this concept, I began to broaden my search for materials, start serious research, and get involved in the world of academia.

Thank you, L.A. as Subject! The professional librarians, archivists, and museum personnel of this wonderful organization warmly welcomed me, a dilettante, as one of their own. I have tremendous respect for the professions of librarian, archivist, and curator. Special thanks to Kenn Bicknell, Michael Palmer, Liza Posas, and Dale Stieber.

I am also indebted and grateful to the Citrus Label Society. The knowledge of its members is astounding, exceeded only by their willingness to share. Thank you, Tom Spellman, Jim Campos, and Noel Gilbert.

My deep and sincere appreciation goes to these organizations and people for their invaluable help: the wonderful and enormously talented Amy Inouye and Future Studio (!); John Caragozian, Russ Hanlin, Sr., Chris Martinez and Claire Smith at Sunkist Growers, Inc.; Wally Shidler; Tyson Gaskill, Nathan Masters and Dace Taube of the University of Southern California Libraries; Bill Hahn; Faye Thompson at the Margaret Herrick Library, Academy of Motion Picture Arts and Sciences; Chris Jepsen, assistant archivist at the Orange County Archives; John Bwarie, Los Angeles History Alliance; and the Special Collections Resource Center of the Syracuse University Library.

I'd have no one to thank if it were not for the amazingly supportive, exacting, nurturing, professional, wonderful people at Angel City Press: Paddy Calistro, Scott McAuley, Terri Accomazzo, Lynn Relfe, and Jim Schneeweis.

For their steadfast friendship and extraordinary support, thank you: Camille Argus, Cliff Boulé, Larry Erickson, Samantha Fernandez (my first review!), Joe Hartnett, Joe Martinez (the proposal and more), Molly Mason, Claudia McGee, my mother Iris Miller, Andrew Posey, Jill Prestup, Diane Salter, Bill Salter, Mike Shaw, Tony Thacker, David Young-Wolff, and Pam Young-Wolff. I trust that each of you know what a significant and cherished role you played in this endeavor.

And lastly, and especially, thank you and humungous love to my wife Marcia and our son Henry.

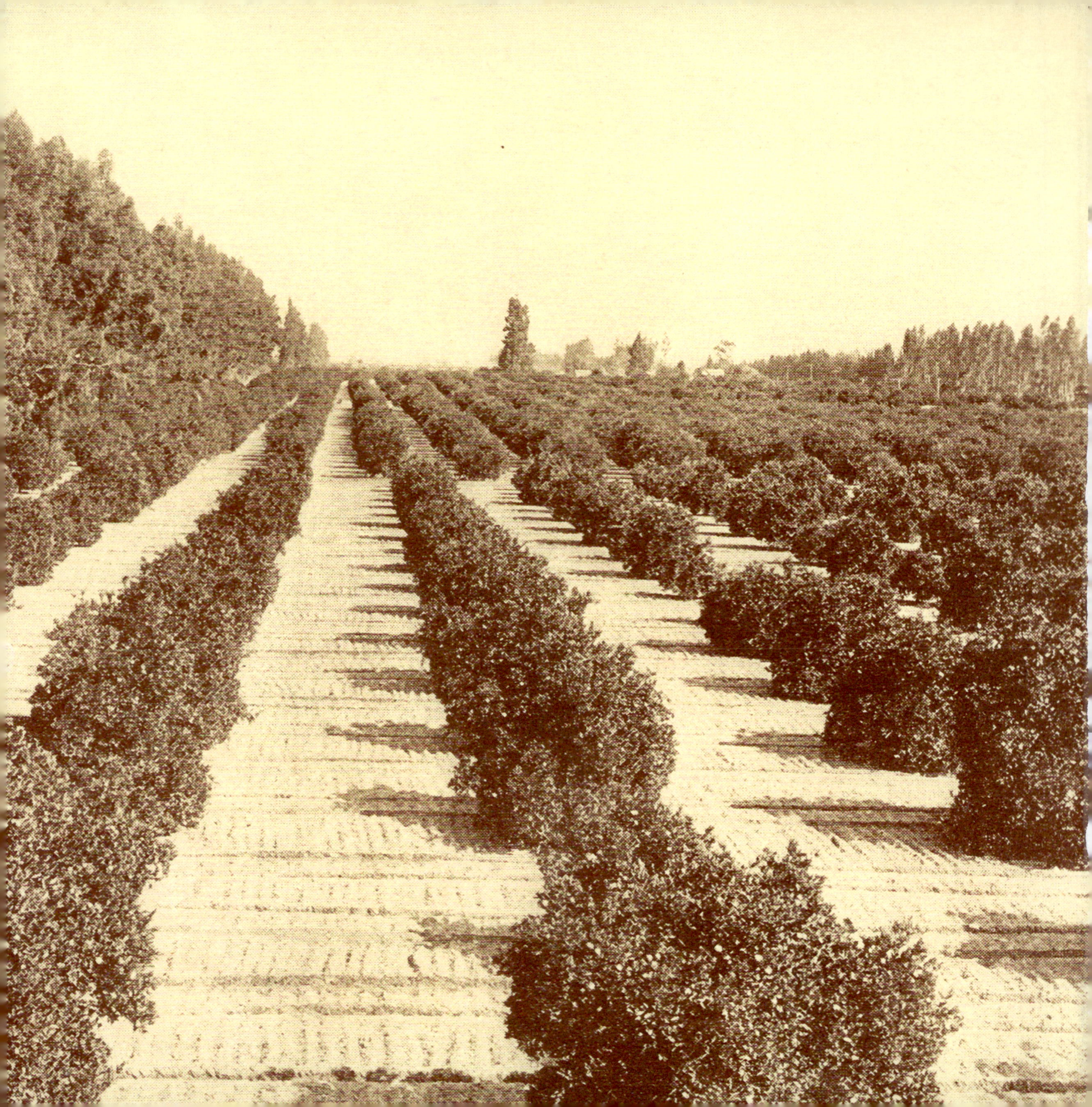

> Reaching for
> stretch the o
> deep green, tinged with
> and lashed into sparkl
> cream of the myriads of
> rises as sweet-smelling
> —GEORGE V
> *Heroes of C*

> Not so many years ag
> fruit, obtainable . . .
> and regarded as a deli
> be put in the C
> of good litt
> —STUAR
> *California—Magaz*